D0417341

Note by the Editor

This volume presents the full text of the Code of Liberalisation of Capital Movements under which OECD members have accepted legally binding obligations. The Code is regularly updated by Decisions of the OECD Council. This edition reflects all changes in the positions of members up to 27 March 2003. It serves as a reference manual to the obligations of members under the Code and to the degree of liberalisation achieved by each member country in regard to capital movements.

The publication *Forty Years' Experience with the OECD Code of Liberalisation of Capital Movements*, OECD (2002), provides an account of the liberalisation process in respective OECD member countries over time.

OECD Codes of Liberalisation: User's Guide, OECD (2003), provides an easily accessible summary of the Codes' principles, as well as technical commentary to the understandings and interpretations developed in their implementation.

Further information about OECD international investment instruments, including regular updates to the reservations of member countries, is available on the website www.oecd.org/daf/investment/instruments.

OECD Code of Liberalisation of Capital Movements

2003

OECD

ORGANISATION FOR ECONOMIC CO-OPERATION AND DEVELOPMENT

9017701

ORGANISATION FOR ECONOMIC CO-OPERATION AND DEVELOPMENT

Pursuant to Article 1 of the Convention signed in Paris on 14th December 1960, and which came into force on 30th September 1961, the Organisation for Economic Co-operation and Development (OECD) shall promote policies designed:

- to achieve the highest sustainable economic growth and employment and a rising standard of living in member countries, while maintaining financial stability, and thus to contribute to the development of the world economy;
- to contribute to sound economic expansion in member as well as non-member countries in the process of economic development; and
- to contribute to the expansion of world trade on a multilateral, non-discriminatory basis in accordance with international obligations.

The original member countries of the OECD are Austria, Belgium, Canada, Denmark, France, Germany, Greece, Iceland, Ireland, Italy, Luxembourg, the Netherlands, Norway, Portugal, Spain, Sweden, Switzerland, Turkey, the United Kingdom and the United States. The following countries became members subsequently through accession at the dates indicated hereafter: Japan (28th April 1964), Finland (28th January 1969), Australia (7th June 1971), New Zealand (29th May 1973), Mexico (18th May 1994), the Czech Republic (21st December 1995), Hungary (7th May 1996), Poland (22nd November 1996), Korea (12th December 1996) and the Slovak Republic (14th December 2000). The Commission of the European Communities takes part in the work of the OECD (Article 13 of the OECD Convention).

Publié en français sous le titre :

Code de l'OCDE de la libération des mouvements de capitaux

2003

TABLE OF CONTENTS

Part III
Terms of Reference

Part IV
Miscellaneous

Annex A
Liberalisation Lists of Capital Movements

Annex B

Annex C

Annex D

Annex E

PREAMBLE

THE COUNCIL,

Having regard to Articles 2 (d) and 5 (a) of the Convention on the Organisation for Economic Co-operation and Development of 14th December 1960;

Having regard to the Code of Liberalisation of Current Invisible Operations;

Having regard to the Articles of Agreement of the International Monetary Fund of 27th December 1945;

Having regard to the European Monetary Agreement of 5th August 1955, and the Protocol of Provisional Application of that Agreement of the same date;

Having regard to the Report of the Committee for Invisible Transactions on the Codes of Liberalisation of Current Invisibles and of Capital Movements of 28th October 1961, and the Comments by the Executive Committee on that Report of 8th December 1961 [OECD/C(61)37; OECD/C(61)73];

DECIDES:

Part I

UNDERTAKINGS WITH REGARD TO CAPITAL MOVEMENTS

Article 1

General Undertakings

a. Members shall progressively abolish between one another, in accordance with the provisions of Article 2, restrictions on movements of capital to the extent necessary for effective economic co-operation. Measures designed to eliminate such restrictions are hereinafter called "measures of liberalisation".

b. Members shall, in particular, endeavour:

  i) to treat all non-resident-owned assets in the same way irrespective of the date of their formation, and

  ii) to permit the liquidation of all non-resident-owned assets and the transfer of such assets or of their liquidation proceeds.

c. Members should use their best offices to ensure that the measures of liberalisation are applied within their overseas territories.

d. Members shall endeavour to extend the measures of liberalisation to all members of the International Monetary Fund.

e. Members shall endeavour to avoid introducing any new exchange restrictions on the movements of capital or the use of non-resident-owned funds and shall endeavour to avoid making existing regulations more restrictive.

Article 2

Measures of liberalisation

a.　Subject to the provisions of paragraph (b)(iv), Members shall grant any authorisation required for the conclusion or execution of transactions and for transfers specified in an item set out in List A or List B of Annex A to this Code.

b.　A Member may lodge reservations relating to the obligations resulting from paragraph (a) when:

    i)　an item is added to List A of Annex A to this Code;

    ii)　obligations relating to an item in that List are extended;

    iii)　obligations relating to any such item begin to apply to that Member; or

    iv)　at any time, in respect of an item in List B.

Reservations shall be set out in Annex B to the Code.

c.　Whenever the liquidation proceeds of non-resident-owned assets may be transferred, the right of transfer shall include any appreciation of the original assets.

d.　Whenever existing regulations or international agreements permit loans between residents of different Members otherwise than by issuing marketable domestic securities or by using, in the country in which the borrower resides, funds the transfer of which is restricted, the repayment obligation may be expressed or guaranteed in the currency of either of the two Members concerned.

Article 3　Public order and security

The provisions of this Code shall not prevent a Member from taking action which it considers necessary for:

    i)　the maintenance of public order or the protection of public health, morals and safety;

    ii)　the protection of its essential security interests;

    iii)　the fulfilment of its obligations relating to international peace and security.

Article 4

Obligations in existing multilateral international agreements

Nothing in this Code shall be regarded as altering the obligations undertaken by a Member as a Signatory of the Articles of Agreement of the International Monetary Fund or other existing multilateral international agreements.

Article 5

Controls and formalities

a.　The measures of liberalisation provided for in this Code shall not limit the powers of Members to verify the authenticity of transactions or transfers nor to take any measures required to prevent evasion of their laws or regulations.

b.　Members shall simplify as much as possible all formalities connected with the authorisation or verification of transactions or transfers and shall co-operate, if necessary, to attain such simplification.

Article 6

Execution of transfers

A Member shall be deemed to have complied with its obligations as regards transfers whenever a transfer may be made:

i)　between persons entitled, by the exchange regulations of the State from which and of the State to which the transfer is to be made, respectively, to make and/or to receive the said transfer;

ii)　in accordance with international agreements in force at the time the transfer is to be made; and

iii)　in accordance with the monetary arrangements in force between the State from which and the State to which the transfer is to be made.

Article 7

Clauses of derogation

a.   If its economic and financial situation justifies such a course, a Member need not take the whole of the measures of liberalisation provided for in Article 2(a).

b.   If any measures of liberalisation taken or maintained in accordance with the provisions of Article 2(a) result in serious economic and financial disturbance in the Member State concerned, that Member may withdraw those measures.

c.   If the overall balance of payments of a Member develops adversely at a rate and in circumstances, including the state of its monetary reserves, which it considers serious, that member may temporarily suspend the application of measures of liberalisation taken or maintained in accordance with the provisions of Article 2(a).

d.   However, a Member invoking paragraph (c) shall endeavour to ensure that its measures of liberalisation:

   i)   cover, twelve months after it has invoked that paragraph, to a reasonable extent, having regard to the need for advancing towards the objective defined in sub-paragraph ii), transactions and transfers which the Member must authorise in accordance with Article 2(a) and the authorisation of which it has suspended, since it invoked paragraph (c); and

   ii)   comply, eighteen months after it has invoked that paragraph, with its obligations under Article 2(a).

e.   Any Member invoking the provisions of this Article shall do so in such a way as to avoid unnecessary damage which bears especially on the financial or economic interests of another Member and, in particular, shall avoid any discrimination between other Members.

Article 8

Right to benefit from measures of liberalisation

Any Member lodging a reservation under Article 2(b) or invoking the provisions of Article 7 shall, nevertheless, benefit from the measures of liberalisation taken by other Members, provided it has complied with the procedure laid down in Article 12 or Article 13 as the case may be.

Article 9

Non-discrimination

A Member shall not discriminate as between other Members in authorising the conclusion and execution of transactions and transfers which are listed in Annex A and which are subject to any degree of liberalisation.

Article 10

Exceptions to the principle of non-discrimination special customs or monetary systems

Members forming part of a special customs or monetary system may apply to one another, in addition to measures of liberalisation taken in accordance with the provisions of Article 2(a), other measures of liberalisation without extending them to other Members. Members forming part of such a system shall inform the Organisation of its membership and those of its provisions which have a bearing on this Code.

Part II

PROCEDURE

Article 11

Notification and information from members

a.   Members shall notify the Organisation, within the periods which the latter may determine, of the measures of liberalisation which they have taken and of any other measures which have a bearing on this Code, as well as of any modifications of such measures.

b.   Members shall notify the Organisation forthwith of any cases in which they have by virtue of remark *ii)* against Section I of List A of Annex A to this Code imposed restrictions on specific transactions or transfers relating to direct investments and shall state their reasons for doing so.

c.   Members shall submit to the Organisation, at intervals determined by the Organisation, but of no more than eighteen months, information concerning:

    i)   any channels, other than official channels, through which transfers are made, and any rates of exchange applying to such transfers, if they are different from the official rates of exchange;

    ii)   any security money markets and any premiums or discounts in relation to official rates of exchange prevailing therein.

d.   The Organisation shall consider the notifications submitted to it in accordance with the provisions of paragraphs (a), (b) and (c) with a view to determining whether each Member is complying with its obligations under this Code.

15

Article 12

Notification and examination of reservations lodged under article 2(b)

a.   Each Member lodging a reservation in respect of an item specified in List B of Annex A to the Code shall forthwith notify the Organisation of its reasons therefor.

b.   Each Member shall notify the Organisation within a period to be determined by the Organisation, whether it desires to maintain any reservation lodged by it in respect of an item specified in List A or List B of Annex A to this Code, and if so, state its reasons therefor.

c.   The Organisation shall examine each reservation lodged by a Member in respect of an item specified in:

   i)   List A at intervals of not more than eighteen months;

   ii)   List B within six months of notification, and at intervals of not more than eighteen months thereafter;

   unless the Council decides otherwise.

d.   The examinations provided for in paragraph (c) shall be directed to making suitable proposals designed to assist Members to withdraw their reservations.

Article 13

Notification and examination of derogations made under article 7

a.   Any Member invoking the provisions of Article 7 shall notify the Organisation forthwith of its action, together with its reasons therefore.

b.   The Organisation shall consider the notification and reasons submitted to it in accordance with the provisions of paragraph (a) with a view to determining whether the Member concerned is justified in invoking the provisions of Article 7 and, in particular, whether it is complying with the provisions of paragraph (e) of that Article.

c.   If the action taken by a Member in accordance with the provisions of Article 7 is not disapproved by the Organisation, that action shall be reconsidered by the Organisation every six months or, subject to the provisions of Article 15, on any other date which the latter may deem appropriate.

d.   If, however, in the opinion of a Member other than the one which has invoked Article 7, the circumstances justifying the action taken by the latter in accordance with the provisions of that Article have changed, that other Member may at any time refer to the Organisation for reconsideration of the case at issue.

e.   If the action taken by a Member in accordance with the provisions of paragraph (a), (b) or (c) of Article 7 has not been disapproved by the Organisation, then if that Member subsequently invokes paragraph (a), (b) or (c) of Article 7 of the Code of Liberalisation of Current Invisible Operations, or, having invoked one paragraph of Article 7 of this Code, invokes another paragraph of that Article, its case shall be reconsidered by the Organisation after six months have elapsed since the date of the previous consideration, or on any other date which the latter may deem appropriate. If another Member claims that the Member in question is failing to carry out its obligations under paragraph (e) of Article 7 of this Code or paragraph (e) of Article 7 of the Code of Liberalisation of Current Invisible Operations, the Organisation shall consider the case without delay.

f.   i)   If the Organisation, following its consideration in accordance with paragraph (b), determines that a Member is not justified in invoking the provisions of Article 7 or is not complying with the provisions of that Article, it shall remain in consultation with the Member concerned, with a view to restoring compliance with the Code.

ii)   If, after a reasonable period of time, that Member continues to invoke the provisions of Article 7, the Organisation shall reconsider the matter. If the Organisation is then unable to determine that the Member concerned is justified in invoking the provisions of Article 7 or is complying with the provisions of that Article, the situation of that Member shall be examined at a session of the Council convened by its Chairman for this purpose unless the Organisation decides on some other procedure.

Article 14

Examination of derogations made under article 7 members in process of economic development

a.   In examining the case of any Member which it considers to be in the process of economic development and which has invoked the provisions of Article 7 the Organisation shall have special regard to the effect that the economic development of the Member has upon its ability to carry out its obligations under paragraph (a) of Articles 1 and 2.

b. In order to reconcile the obligations of the Member concerned under paragraph (a) of Article 2 with the requirements of its economic development, the Organisation may grant that Member a special dispensation from those obligations.

Article 15

Special report and examination concerning derogations made under article 7

a. A Member invoking the provisions of paragraph (c) of Article 7 shall report to the Organisation, within ten months after such invocation, on the measures of liberalisation it has restored or proposes to restore in order to attain the objective determined in sub-paragraph (d)i) of Article 7. The Member shall, if it continues to invoke these provisions, report to the Organisation again on the same subject - but with reference to the objective determined in sub-paragraph (d)ii) of Article 7 - within sixteen months after such invocation.

b. If the Member considers that it will not be able to attain the objective, it shall indicate its reasons in its report and, in addition, shall state:

i) what internal measures it has taken to restore its economic equilibrium and what results have already been attained, and

ii) what further internal measures it proposes to take and what additional period it considers it will need in order to attain the objective determined in sub-paragraph (d)i) or (d)ii) of Article 7.

c. In cases referred to in paragraph (b), the Organisation shall consider within a period of twelve months, and, if required, of eighteen months from the date on which the Member invoked the provisions of paragraph (c) of Article 7, whether the situation of that Member appears to justify its failure to attain the objective determined in sub-paragraph (d)i) or (d)ii) of Article 7 and whether the measures taken or envisaged and the period considered by it as necessary for attaining the objective determined, appear acceptable in the light of the objectives of the Organisation in the commercial and financial fields.

d. If a Member invokes the provisions of both paragraph (c) of Article 7 of this Code and paragraph (c) of Article 7 of the Code of Liberalisation of Current Invisible Operations, the periods of twelve and eighteen months referred to in paragraph (c) shall run from the date of the earlier invocation.

e.   If following any of the examinations provided for in paragraph (c) the Organisation is unable to approve the arguments advanced by the Member concerned in accordance with the provisions of paragraph (b), the situation of that Member shall be examined at a session of the Council convened by its Chairman for this purpose unless the Organisation decides on some other procedure.

Article 16

Reference to the organisation internal arrangements

a.   If a Member considers that the measures of liberalisation taken or maintained by another Member, in accordance with Article 2(a), are frustrated by internal arrangements likely to restrict the possibility of effecting transactions or transfers, and if it considers itself prejudiced by such arrangements, for instance because of their discriminatory effect, it may refer to the Organisation.

b.   If, following the consideration of a matter referred to it under paragraph (a) the Organisation determines that internal arrangements introduced or maintained by the Member concerned have the effect of frustrating its measures of liberalisation, the Organisation may make suitable suggestions with regard to the removal or modification of such arrangements.

Article 17

Reference to the organisation retention, introduction or reintroduction of restrictions

a.   If a Member considers that another Member which has not invoked the provisions of Article 7 has retained, introduced or reintroduced restrictions on capital movements or the use of non-resident-owned funds contrary to the provisions of Articles 1, 2, 9 or 10, and if it considers itself to be prejudiced thereby, it may refer to the Organisation.

b.   The fact that the case is under consideration by the Organisation shall not preclude the Member which has referred to the Organisation from entering into bilateral conversations on the matter with the other Member concerned.

Part III

TERMS OF REFERENCE

Article 18

Committee on Capital Movements
and Invisible Transactions - General tasks

a.   The Committee on Capital Movements and Invisible Transactions shall consider all questions concerning the interpretation or implementation of the provisions of this Code or other Acts of the Council relating to the liberalisation of capital movements and the use of non-residents-owned funds and shall report its conclusions thereon to the Council as appropriate.

b.   The Committee on Capital Movements and Invisible Transactions shall submit to the Council any appropriate proposals in connection with its tasks as defined in paragraph (a) and, in particular, with the extension of measures of liberalisation as provided in Article 1 of this Code.

Article 19

Committee on Capital Movements
and Invisible Transactions - Special tasks

a.   The Committee on Capital Movements and Invisible Transactions shall:

  i)   determine the periods within which the information provided for in paragraphs (a) and (c) of Article 11 and the reasons provided for in paragraph (b) of Article 12 should be notified to the Organisation by the Members concerned;

  ii)   subject to paragraph (c) of this Article, consider, in conformity with paragraphs (c) and (d) of Article 12, each reservation notified to the Organisation in accordance with paragraphs (a) and (b) of that Article and make, where appropriate, suitable proposals designed to assist Members to withdraw their reservations;

iii) determine, in accordance with the provisions of Article 12, the date on which any reservation should be re-examined, if the reservation has not been withdrawn in the meantime;

iv) consider, in accordance with the provisions of paragraph (d) of Article 11, the notifications submitted to the Organisation;

v) consider reports and references submitted to the Organisation in accordance with the provisions of Article 13 or paragraphs (a) and (b) of Article 15 where a Member has invoked the provisions of Article 7, or submitted in accordance with the provisions of Article 16 or Article 17;

vi) determine the date on which the case of a Member which has invoked Article 7 should be reconsidered in accordance with the provisions of paragraph (c), paragraph (e) or paragraph (f)ii) of Article 13;

vii) transmit to the United States Government, with any comments it considers appropriate, notifications received from Members in accordance with paragraph 2(a) of the Decision in Annex C to the Code; and

viii) consider information received from the United States Government in accordance with paragraph 2(b) of the Decision in Annex C to the Code.

b.   When examining the reservations notified in accordance with paragraph (b) of Article 12, the Committee may, at its discretion, consider together either all reservations made by the same Member or all reservations made in respect of the same item specified in Annex A to this Code.

c.   The Committee shall, however, not consider any reservations notified to the Organisation in accordance with paragraph (b) of Article 12 by a Member which, at the time of the examination in respect of the item subject to that reservation, is invoking the provisions of Article 7 or is enjoying a dispensation in accordance with paragraph (b) of Article 14.

d.   In the cases provided for in sub-paragraphs ii), iv), v) and viii) of paragraph (a), the Committee shall report to the Council, except in cases of notifications under Article 11 (b) on which the Committee shall report only if it considers this appropriate.

e.   The Committee shall, whenever it considers it necessary:

    i)   consult other Committees of the Organisation on any questions relating to the liberalisation of capital movements; and, in particular,

    ii)   request other Committees of the Organisation to give their views on any questions relating to the balance of payments and the state of the monetary reserves of a Member.

Part IV

MISCELLANEOUS

Article 20

Definitions

In this Code:

i) "Member" shall mean a Member of the Organisation which adheres to this Code;

ii) "Domestic securities" shall mean securities issued or to be issued by a resident;

iii) "Foreign securities" shall mean securities issued or to be issued by a non-resident;

iv) "Recognised security market" shall mean a stock exchange or security market in a Member country (including an over-the-counter market organised by a recognised association of security dealers);

- which is officially recognised in the country where it operates;
- on which the public can buy and sell securities; and
- on which dealings take place in accordance with fixed rules;

v) "Securities quoted on a recognised security market" shall mean securities which have been granted an official quotation or are officially listed on such a market or for which dealing prices on such a market are published not less frequently than once a week;

vi) Security dealing on a "spot basis" shall mean dealing with payment and delivery to be made immediately the transaction is concluded or on the next periodic settlement date of the stock exchange where the transaction takes place;

vii) "Money market securities" shall mean securities with an original maturity of less than one year;

viii) "Collective investment securities" shall mean the share certificates, registry entries or other evidence of investor interest in an institution for collective investment which, irrespective of legal form, is organised for the purpose of managing investments in securities or in other assets, applies the principle of risk-spreading, issues its own securities to the public on demand either continuously or at frequent intervals and is required on the request of the holder to redeem such securities, directly or indirectly, within a specified period and at their net asset value;

ix) "Financial institutions" shall mean banks, savings banks, bodies which specialise in the granting of credits, insurance companies, building societies, investment companies, and other establishments of a similar nature;

x) "Deposit" shall mean a sum of money paid on terms: a) under which it will be repaid, with or without interest or premium, and either on demand or at a time or in circumstances agreed by the person making it or receiving it or by his order, and b) which are not referable to the provision of property or services or to the giving of security;

xi) "Official channels" shall mean foreign exchange markets in which an officially established rate or officially established rates apply and in which spot transactions take place at rates which are free to fluctuate within the official margins;

xii) "Blocked funds" shall mean funds owned by residents of other Member countries in accordance with the laws and regulations of the Member where the funds are held and blocked for balance-of-payments reasons;

xiii) "Unit of account" shall mean the sum in the national currency of a Member which is equal to a unit of value of special drawing rights as valued by the International Monetary Fund.

Article 21

Title of decision

This Decision, referred to in the present text as the "Code", shall be known as the "Code of Liberalisation of Capital Movements".

Article 22

Withdrawal

Any Member may withdraw from the Code by transmitting a notice in writing to the Secretary-General of the Organisation. The withdrawal shall become effective twelve months from the date on which such notice is received.

Annex A

LIBERALISATION LISTS OF CAPITAL MOVEMENTS[1]

LIST A

I. Direct Investment

Investment for the purpose of establishing lasting economic relations with an undertaking such as, in particular, investments which give the possibility of exercising an effective influence on the management thereof:

A. In the country concerned by non-residents by means of:

    1. Creation or extension of a wholly-owned enterprise, subsidiary or branch, acquisition of full ownership of an existing enterprise;

    2. Participation in a new or existing enterprise;

    3. A loan of five years or longer.

B. Abroad by residents by means of:

    1. Creation or extension of a wholly-owned enterprise, subsidiary or branch, acquisition of full ownership of an existing enterprise;

    2. Participation in a new or existing enterprise;

    3. A loan of five years or longer.

Remarks: Transactions and transfers under A and B shall be free unless:

    i) An investment is of a purely financial character designed only to gain for the investor indirect access to the money or financial market of another country; or ii)   *In view of the amount involved or of other factors a specific transaction or transfer would have an exceptionally detrimental effect on the interests of the Member concerned.*

The authorities of Members shall not maintain or introduce:

Regulations or practices applying to the granting of licences, concessions, or similar authorisations, including conditions or requirements attaching to such authorisations and affecting the operations of enterprises, that raise special barriers or limitations with respect to non-resident (as compared to resident) investors, and that have the intent or the effect of preventing or significantly *impeding inward direct investment by non-residents.*

II. Liquidation of direct investment

A.   Abroad by residents.

B.   In the country concerned by non-residents.

III. Operations in real estate[2]

A.   Operations in the country concerned by non-residents:

       1.   (See List B)

       2.   Sale.

B.   Operations abroad by residents:

       1.   (See List B)

       2.   Sale.

IV. Operations in securities on capital markets[3]

A.   Admission of domestic securities on a foreign capital market:

1. Issue through placing or public sale of

     a)   shares or other securities of a participating nature;

2. Introduction on a recognised domestic security market of

     b)   bonds and other debt securities (original maturity of one year or more).

B.   Admission of foreign securities on the domestic capital market:

1. Issue through placing or   a) shares or other securities of a
    public sale of   participating nature;

2. Introduction on a   b) bonds   and   other   debt
    recognised domestic   securities (original maturity
    security market of   of one year or more).

C.   Operations in the country concerned by non-residents:

1. Purchase   a) shares   or   other   securities   of   a
                                          participating nature;
2. Sale
                                      b) bonds and other debt securities (original
                                          maturity of one year or more).

D.   Operations abroad by residents:

1. Purchase   a) shares   or   other   securities   of   a
                                          participating nature;
2. Sale
                                      b) bonds and other debt securities (original
                                          maturity of one year or more).

Remarks: The liberalisation obligations under B1 and B2 are subject to the regulations of the security markets concerned. The authorities of Members shall not maintain or introduce restrictions which discriminate against foreign securities.

Members may:

a)   With regard to transactions and transfers under A, B, C and D require that:

   i)   Such transactions and transfers must be carried out through authorised resident agents;
   ii) In connection with such transactions and transfers residents may hold funds and securities only through the intermediary of such agents; and
   iii) Purchases and sales may be contracted only on a spot basis;

b)   With regard to transactions and transfers under C2, take measures for the protection of investors, including the regulation of promotional activities, provided such measures do not discriminate against the residents of any other Member;

c)   *With regard to transactions and transfers under D1, regulate on their territory any promotional activities by, or on behalf of, the residents of other Members.*

V. Operations on money markets[4]

(See List B)

VI. Other operations in negotiable instruments and non-securitised claims[5]

(See List B)

VII. Operations in collective investment securities

A.   Admission of domestic collective investment securities on a foreign securities market:

1.   Issue through placing or public sale.

2.   Introduction on a recognised foreign securities market.

B.   Admission of foreign collective investment securities on the domestic securities market:

1.   Issue through placing or public sale.

2.   Introduction on a recognised domestic securities market.

C.   Operations in the country concerned by non-residents:

1.   Purchase.

2.   Sale.

D.   Operations abroad by residents:

1.   Purchase.

2.   Sale.

Remarks: The liberalisation obligations under B1 and B2 are subject to the regulations of the security markets concerned.

The authorities of Members shall not maintain or introduce restrictions which discriminate against foreign collective investment securities.

Members may:

a) *With regard to transactions and transfers under A, B, C and D require that:*

   i) *Such transactions and transfers must be carried out through authorised resident agents;*
   ii) *In connection with such transactions and transfers residents may hold funds and securities only through the intermediary of such agents; and*
   iii) *Purchases and sales may be contracted only on a spot basis;*

b) *With regard to transactions and transfers under C2, take measures for the protection of investors, including the regulation of promotional activities, provided such measures do not discriminate against institutions for collective investment organised under the laws of any other Member;*

c) *With regard to transactions and transfers under D1, regulate on their territory any promotional activities of foreign institutions for collective investment.*

VIII. Credits directly linked with international commercial transactions or with the rendering of international services

   i) In cases where a resident participates in the underlying commercial or service transaction.

A. Credits granted by non-residents to residents.

B. Credits granted by residents to non-residents.

   ii) In cases where no resident participates in the underlying commercial or service transaction.

(See List B)

IX. Financial credits and loans[6]

(See List B)

X. Sureties, guarantees and financial back-up facilities

    i)   In cases directly related to international trade or international current invisible operations, or in cases related to international capital movement operations in which a resident participates.

A.   Sureties and guarantees:

    1.   By non-residents in favour of residents.

    2.   By residents in favour of non-residents.

B.   Financial back-up facilities:

    1.   By non-residents in favour of residents.

    2.   By residents in favour of non-residents.

Remark: Transactions and transfers under X(i)A and B shall be free if they are directly related to international trade, international current invisible operations or international capital movement operations in which a resident participates and which do not require authorisation or have been authorised by the Member concerned.

    ii)   In cases not directly related to international trade, international current invisible operations or international capital movement operations, or where no resident participates in the underlying international operation concerned.

A.   Sureties and guarantees:

    1.   By non-residents in favour of residents.

    2.   By residents in favour of non-residents.

B.   Financial back-up facilities:
    (See List B)

XI. Operation of deposit accounts[7]

A.   Operation by non-residents of accounts with resident institutions:

    1.   In domestic currency.

    2.   In foreign currency.

B. Operation by residents of accounts with non-resident institutions:

(See List B)

Remark: Transactions and transfers under XI/A shall be free provided the deposit accounts are operated with financial institutions authorised to accept deposits.

XII. Operations in foreign exchange[8]

(See List B)

XIII. Life assurance

Capital transfers arising under life assurance contracts[9]:

A. Transfers of capital and annuities certain due to resident beneficiaries from non-resident insurers.

B. Transfers of capital and annuities certain due to non-resident beneficiaries from resident insurers.

Remark: Transfers under A and B shall be free also in the case of contracts under which the persons from whom premiums are due or the beneficiaries to whom disbursements are due were residents of the same country as the insurer at the time of the conclusion of the contract but have changed their residence since.

XIV. Personal capital movements

A. Loans.

B. Gifts and endowments.

C. Dowries.

D. Inheritances and legacies.

Remark: Transfers under D shall be free provided that the deceased was resident and the beneficiary non-resident at the time of the deceased's death.

E. Settlement of debts in their country of origin by immigrants.

F.   Emigrants' assets.

Remark: Transfers under F shall be free upon emigration irrespective of the nationality of the emigrant.

G.   Gaming.

(See List B)

H.   Savings of non-resident workers.

XV. Physical movement of capital assets

A.   Securities and other documents of title to capital assets:

      1.   Import.

      2.   Export.

B.   Means of payment:

      1.   Import.

      2.   Export.

Remark: In the case of residents the obligation to permit an export applies only to the export of foreign securities and then only on a temporary basis for administrative purposes.

XVI. Disposal of non-resident-owned blocked funds

A.   Transfer of blocked funds.

B.   Use of blocked funds in the country concerned:

      1.   For operations of a capital nature.

      2.   For current operations.

C.   Cession of blocked funds between non-residents.

LIST B[10]

III. Operations in real estate[11]

A.   Operations in the country concerned by non-residents:

      1.   Building or purchase.

      2.   (See List A)

B.   Operations abroad by residents:

      1.   Building or purchase.

      2.   (Scc List A)

V. Operations on money markets[12]

A.   Admission of domestic securities and other instruments on a foreign money market:

      1.   Issue through placing or public sale.

      2.   Introduction on a recognised foreign money market.

B.   Admission of foreign securities and other instruments on the domestic money market:

      1.   Issue through placing or public sale.

      2.   Introduction on a recognised domestic money market.

C.   Operations in the country concerned by non-residents:

      1.   Purchase of money market securities.

      2.   Sale of money market securities.

      3.   Lending through other money market instruments.

      4.   Borrowing through other money market instruments.

D.   Operations abroad by residents:

      1.   Purchase of money market securities.

      2.   Sale of money market securities.

      3.   Lending through other money market instruments.

      4.   Borrowing through other money market instruments.

Remarks: The liberalisation obligations under B1 and B2 are subject to the regulations of the security markets concerned.

The authorities of Members shall not maintain or introduce restrictions which discriminate against foreign money market securities or other money market instruments.

Members may:

a) *With regard to transactions and transfers under A, B, C and D require that:*

    i) *Such transactions and transfers must be carried out through authorised resident agents;*

    ii) *In connection with such transactions and transfers residents may hold funds, securities and other instruments only through the intermediary of such agents; and*

    iii) *Purchases and sales may be contracted only on a spot basis;*

b) *With regard to transactions and transfers under C2, take measures for the protection of investors, including the regulation of promotional activities, provided such measures do not discriminate against the residents of any other Member;*

c) *With regard to transactions and transfers under D1, regulate on their territory any promotional activities, by or on behalf of, the residents of other Members.*

VI. Other operations in negotiable instruments and non-securitised claims[13]

A.   Admission of domestic instruments and claims on a foreign financial market:

    1.   Issue through placing or public sale.

    2.   Introduction on a recognised foreign financial market.

B.   Admission of foreign instruments and claims on a domestic financial market:

    1.   Issue through placing or public sale.

    2.   Introduction on a recognised domestic financial market.

C.   Operations in the country concerned by non-residents.

      1.   Purchase.

      2.   Sale.

      3.   Exchange for other assets.

D.   Operations abroad by residents:

      1.   Purchase.

      2.   Sale.

      3.   Exchange for other assets.

Remarks: The liberalisation obligations under B1 and B2 are subject to the regulations of the financial markets concerned.

The authorities of Members shall not maintain or introduce restrictions which discriminate against foreign negotiable instruments or non-securitised claims.

Members may:

    a)   With regard to transactions and transfers under A, B, C and D require that:

        i)   Such transactions and transfers must be carried out through authorised resident agents; and

        ii) In connection with such transactions and transfers residents may hold funds, negotiable instruments and non-securitised claims only through the intermediary of such agents;

    b)   With regard to transactions and transfers under C2 and C3, take measures for the protection of investors, including the regulation of promotional activities, provided such measures do not discriminate against the residents of any other Member;

    c)   With regard to transactions and transfers under D1 and D3, regulate on their territory any promotional activities by, or on behalf of, the residents of other Members.

VIII. Credits directly linked with international commercial transactions or with the rendering of international services

i) In cases where a resident participates in the underlying commercial or service transaction.
(See List A)

ii) In cases where no resident participates in the underlying commercial or service transaction.

A. -

B. Credits granted by residents to non-residents.

Remark: Transactions and transfers under VIII(ii)/B shall be free if the creditor is an enterprise permitted to extend credits and loans on its national market.

IX. Financial credits and loans[14]

A. Credits and loans granted by non-residents to residents.

B. Credits and loans granted by residents to non-residents.

Remarks: Transactions and transfers under IX/A shall be free if the debtor is an enterprise.

Transactions and transfers under IX/B shall be free if the creditor is an enterprise permitted to extend credits and loans on its national market.

X. Sureties, guarantees and financial back-up facilities

i) In cases directly related to international trade or international current invisible operations, or in cases related to international capital movement operations in which a resident participates.

(See List A)

ii) In cases not directly related to international trade, international current invisible operations, or international capital movement operations, or where no resident participates in the underlying international operation concerned.

A. Sureties and guarantees:

(See List A)

B.   Financial back-up facilities:

    1.   By non-residents in favour of residents.

    2.   By residents in favour of non-residents.

XI. Operation of deposit accounts[15]

A.   Operation by non-residents of accounts with resident institutions: (See List A)

B.   Operation by residents of accounts with non-resident institutions:

    1.   In domestic currency.

    2.   In foreign currency.

XII. Operations in foreign exchange[16]

A.   In the country concerned by non-residents:

    1.   Purchase of domestic currency with foreign currency.

    2.   Sale of domestic currency for foreign currency.

    3.   Exchange of foreign currencies.

B.   Abroad by residents:

    1.   Purchase of foreign currency with domestic currency.

    2.   Sale of foreign currency for domestic currency.

    3.   Exchange of foreign currencies.

Remark: Transactions and transfers under XII/A and B shall be free provided the operations are carried out through authorised resident agents.

XIV. Personal capital movements

A. to F. (See List A)

G.   Gaming.

Remark: Transfers under G shall be free only in respect of winnings. The provision does not cover the stakes wagered.

H.   (See List A)

Notes and references to Annex A

1. All items in the General List of International Capital Movements and Certain Related Operations (see Annex D to the Code) appear on either List A or List B in this Annex A.

2. Other than operations falling under Sections I or II of the General List.

3. Other than operations falling under Section IV of the General List.

4. Other than operations falling under Section IV of the General List.

5. Other than operations falling under Sections IV, V or VII of the General List.

6. Other than credits and loans falling under Sections I, II, VIII or XIV of the General List.

7. Other than operations falling under Section V of the General List.

8. Other than operations falling under any other Section of the General List.

9. Transfers of premiums and pensions and annuities, other than annuities certain, in connection with life assurance contracts are governed by the Code of Liberalisation of Current Invisible Operations (Item D/3). Transfers of whatever kind or size under other than life assurance contracts are always considered to be of a current nature and are consequently governed by the Current Invisibles Code.

10. All items in the General List of International Capital Movements and Certain Related Operations (see Annex D to the Code) appear on either List A or List B in this Annex A.

11. Other than operations falling under Sections I or II of the General List.

12. Other than operations falling under Section IV of the General List.

13. Other than operations falling under Sections IV, V or VII of the General List.

14. Other than credits and loans falling under Sections I, II, VIII or XIV of the General List.

15. Other than operations falling under Section V of the General List.

16. Other than operations falling under any other Section of the General List.

AUSTRALIA

Annex B

RESERVATIONS TO THE CODE OF LIBERALISATION
OF CAPITAL MOVEMENTS

The present Annex contains the reservations that individual Member countries have lodged in accordance with Article 2 (b) to the Code. The reservations have been accepted by the Council and constitute authority for Members to derogate, from the provisions of Article 2 (a) of the Code with regard to transactions and transfers enumerated in the Liberalisation Lists A and B.

Reservations on items in List A will be withdrawn as Members are able to accept the liberalisation obligations under such items; additional reservations may not be lodged on List A items. Reservations on items in List B may also be withdrawn; additional reservations may be lodged if need be. The present Annex will be amended accordingly by Decisions of the Council, as the need arises.

In the country pages that follow, the asterisks added to the mention of item I/A of List A refer to measures or practices, described in Annex E thereafter, allowing inward direct investment or establishment under conditions of reciprocity (i.e. allowing residents of another Member country to invest or establish in the Member country concerned under terms similar to those applied by the other Member country to investors resident in the Member country concerned) and/or involving discrimination among investors originating in various OECD Member countries (other than the exceptions to the principle of non-discrimination referred to in Article 10 of the Code of Liberalisation of Capital Movements). Annex E also includes a Council Decision relating to these measures and practices.

Where Member countries permit or prescribe that payment in connection with certain items be made by means other than transfer through the official foreign exchange market, such restrictions would be recorded under "Notes concerning Payments Channels". No Member country presently maintains restrictions concerning payments channels.

AUSTRALIA

General Remark: The Australian Government accepts the enlarged obligations on banking and financial services in the Code of Liberalisation of Capital Movements consistent with its constitutional powers and the reservations it has lodged in respect of some of the enlarged obligations.

Bearing in mind that the Australian Constitution provides for a federal system of government and State and Territory Governments have powers in relation to some matters within the scope of the enlarged obligations, Australia reserves its position in respect of the enlarged obligations insofar as these obligations relate to actions, including any action in relation to taxation, undertaken by Australian State or Territory Governments. This applies to the enlarged obligations under Items IV to XII, XV and XVI of the Revised Capital Movements Code.

The Australian authorities will take steps to encourage the States and Territories to achieve the liberalisation of operations covered by the enlarged obligations of the Codes that fall within their jurisdiction and will call their attention to the basic principles underlying the liberalisation obligations under the Code. The Australian authorities will also seek the co-operation of the States and Territories in providing information on any existing restrictions applied at the State or Territory level, as well as any new measures that might be taken at that level.

In the event that a Member of the OECD considers that its interests under the Codes are being prejudiced by the actions of an Australian State or Territory Government, the Australian authorities will consult with the Member and the State or Territory Government concerned. They will bring the provisions of the Code and the circumstances of the case in question to the attention of the competent authorities of any State or Territory concerned together with an appropriate recommendation. They will also inform the Organisation of the action taken in this regard and of the results thereof.

*List B,   Direct investment:

I/A
  – In the country concerned by non-residents.

   Remark: The reservation applies only to:

   i) *Investments in banking, real estate, mass circulation and ethnic newspapers, broadcasting (including television), civil aviation and uranium;*

ii) Proposals falling within the scope of Australia's Foreign Acquisitions and Take-overs Act 1975, which broadly covers acquisitions of urban land, acquisitions of partial or controlling interests in Australian companies or businesses with total assets valued over US$ 50 million and other arrangements relating to foreign control of companies and businesses;

iii) Proposals to establish new businesses or projects where the total investment is A$ 10 million or more;

iv) Investments by foreign governments or their agencies;

v) Investments to the extent that constituent States or Territories of Australia exercise legislative and administrative control over such investment;

vi) Ownership of Australian flag vessels, except through an enterprise incorporated in Australia.

List B,
III/A1

Operations in real estate:

- In the country concerned by non-residents.

Remark: The reservation does not apply to:

i) Acquisitions of direct interests in non-residential commercial real estate valued under $5 million or $50 million where such real estate is not heritage listed;

ii) Acquisitions of interests in time-share schemes where the entitlement of the foreign interest and any associates is less than four weeks per year;

iii) Acquisitions of residential real estate by approved migrants, special category visa holders, and other foreign nationals entitled to permanent residence in Australia, including Australian permanent residents, not ordinarily resident in Australia and special category visa holders buying through Australian companies and trusts;

iv) Acquisitions by non-resident Australian citizens, either directly or indirectly through Australian companies and trusts;

v) *Acquisitions of offices and residences by foreign government missions for use as official missions or residences for staff subject to sale to Australians or other eligible purchasers when no longer being used for those purposes;*

vi) *Acquisitions of minority interests in public companies and trusts whose principal assets are comprised of real estate, to the extent permitted by regulations under the Foreign Acquisitions and Take-overs Act;*

vii) *Acquisitions of real estate by general insurance companies operating in Australia where the acquisitions are made from the reserves of the companies and are within the prudential guidelines of the Insurance Commissioner;*

viii) *Acquisitions by life assurance companies, representing investment of their Australian statutory funds, by Australian pension funds of foreign employers and by foreign-controlled charities or charitable trusts operating in Australia for the primary benefit of Australians;*

ix) *Acquisitions of strata-titled hotel rooms in designated hotels where each room is subject to a long-term hotel agreement;*

x) *Acquisitions of residential real estate by Australian citizens and their foreign spouses where they purchase as joint tenants;*

xi) *Acquisitions of Australian urban land by foreign owned responsible entities acting on behalf of managed unit trusts and other public investment schemes registered under Chapter 5C of the Corporations Law, where they are investing for the benefit of fund investors or unit holders ordinarily resident in Australia.*

List A, IV/B1, B2   Operations in securities on capital markets:

- Issue through placing or public sale of foreign securities on the domestic capital market.

Remark: The reservation applies only to the issue of bearer securities by foreign central banks, foreign governments, foreign government agencies not akin to private sector commercial entities, and international governmental organisations.

- Introduction of foreign securities on a recognised domestic security market.

   Remark: The reservation applies only to the issue of bearer securities by foreign central banks, foreign governments, foreign government agencies not akin to private sector commercial entities, and international governmental organisations.

List B,
V/B1,
B2

Operations on money markets:

- Issue through placing or public sale of foreign securities and other instruments on the domestic money market.

   Remark: The reservation applies only to the issue of bearer securities by foreign central banks, foreign governments, foreign government agencies not akin to private sector commercial entities, and international governmental organisations.

- Introduction of foreign securities and other instruments on a recognised domestic money market.

   Remark: The reservation applies only to the issue of bearer securities by foreign central banks, foreign governments, foreign government agencies not akin to private sector commercial entities, and international governmental organisations.

List B,
VI/B1,
B2

Other operations in negotiable instruments and non-securitised claims:

- Issue through placing or public sale of foreign instruments and claims on a domestic financial market.

   Remark: The reservation applies only to the issue of bearer securities by foreign central banks, foreign governments, foreign government agencies not akin to private sector commercial entities, and international governmental organisations.

- Introduction of foreign instruments and claims on a recognised domestic financial market.

   Remark: The reservation applies only to the issue of bearer securities by foreign central banks, foreign governments, foreign government agencies not akin to private sector commercial entities, and international governmental organisations.

AUSTRIA

*List A,　Direct investment:
I/A
　　　　　－　In the country concerned by non-residents.

　　　　　　Remark: The reservation applies only to:

　　　　　　i)　　*real estate to the extent that the authorities of the Länder have the right to restrict the acquisition of real estate;*

　　　　　　ii)　*auditing;*

　　　　　　iii)　*investment by non-EC residents in accountancy services exceeding 49 per cent;*

　　　　　　iv)　*investment by non-EC nationals in legal services and in engineering and architectural services exceeding 49 per cent;*

　　　　　　v)　　*energy;*

　　　　　　vi)　*transport;*

　　　　　　vii)　*acquisition of 25 per cent or more in ships registered in Austria.*

List B,　Operations in real estate:
III/A1,
B1　　　　－　In the country concerned by non-residents.

　　　　　　Remark:　The reservation applies only to the extent that the authorities of Federal Provinces have the right to restrict the acquisition of real estate.

　　　　　－　Building or purchase abroad by residents.

　　　　　　Remark: the reservation applies to:

　　　　　　i)　　*the acquisition of real estate abroad if the asset in question is to form part of the guarantee funds of a local branch of a non-EC insurance* company *established in Austria;*

　　　　　　ii)　*the acquisition of real* estate *outside the EC if the asset in question is to form part of the cover of the prescribed solvency margin for the local branch of a non-EC insurance company established in Austria or is to form part of the cover of technical reserves of resident insurance companies;*

48

	iii) *the acquisition of real estate* assets *outside Austria by a private pension* fund, *exceeding 10 per cent of its total assets.*
List A, IV/DI	Operations in securities on capital markets:

– Purchase abroad by residents.

Remark: the reservation applies to:

i)   *purchases of securities not denominated in euro currencies by a private pension fund which would cause its total assets not denominated in euro currencies to exceed 50 per cent of its total assets;*

ii)   *purchases of shares not denominated in euro currencies by a private pension fund which would cause such assets to exceed 30 per cent of its total assets.*

List B, V/D1   Operations on money markets:

– Purchase of money market securities abroad by residents.

Remark: the reservation applies to purchases of money market securities not denominated in euro currencies by a private pension fund which would cause its total assets not denominated in euro currencies to exceed 50 per cent of its total assets.

List B, VI/D1   Other operations in negotiable instruments and non-securitised claims:

– Purchase abroad by residents.

Remark: the reservation applies to purchase of or swap operations in instruments and claims not denominated in euro currencies by a private pension fund which would cause its total assets not denominated in euro currencies to exceed 50 per cent of its total assets.

List A, VII/D1	Operations in collective investment securities: – Purchase abroad by residents.

Remark: the reservation applies to:

   i)   *the purchase by an insurance company of collective investment securities issued by non EC-residents if these assets are to form part of its technical reserves (other than those for unit-linked life assurance contracts);*

   ii)   *the purchase of collective investment securities not denominated in euro currencies by a private pension fund which would cause its total assets not denominated in euros to exceed 50 per cent of its total assets;*

   iii)   *the purchase of equity-based collective investment securities not denominated in euro currencies by a private pension fund which would cause such assets to exceed 30 per cent of its total assets.*

List B, IX/B	Financial credits and loans: – Credits and loans granted by residents to non-residents.

Remark: the reservation applies to:

   i)   *loans granted to non-residents or for which the designated collateral is located abroad if the asset in question is to form part of the guarantee funds of a local branch of a non-EC insurance company established in Austria;*

   ii)   *loans granted to residents outside the EC or for which the designated collateral is located outside the EC, if the asset in question is to form part of the cover of the prescribed solvency margin for the local branch of a non-EC insurance company established in Austria or is to form part of the cover of technical reserves of resident insurance companies;*

   iii)   *loans granted in currencies other than euro by private pension funds which would cause its total assets not denominated in euro currencies to exceed 50 per cent of its total assets.*

List B, XI/B2	Operation of deposit accounts: – By residents in foreign currency with non-resident institutions.

Remark: the reservation applies to deposits not denominated in euro currencies by a private pension fund which would cause its total assets not denominated in euro currencies to exceed 50 per cent of its total assets.

BELGIUM

*List A, Direct investment:
I/A
- In the country concerned by non-residents.

   Remark: The reservation applies only to:

    i)   the acquisition of Belgian flag vessels by shipping companies not having their principal office in Belgium;

    ii)   investment by non-EC nationals in accountancy and legal services.

List A,   Operations in securities on capital markets:
IV/DI
- Purchase abroad by residents.

   Remark: the reservation applies to:

    i)   securities not traded on a regulated market negotiable within a period exceeding 3 months, excepting securities issued by financial institutions headquartered in the EC, if these assets are to form part of the cover of the technical reserves of an insurance company or of the assets representative of the liabilities of a private pension fund;

    ii)   securities not traded on a regulated market negotiable within a period exceeding 3 months issued by financial institutions headquartered in the EC, if these assets are to form more than 20 per cent of the cover of the technical reserves of an insurance company or of the assets representative of the liabilities of a private pension fund;

    iii)   securities not traded on a regulated market negotiable within a period not exceeding 3 months, excepting securities issued by financial institutions headquartered in the EC, if these assets are to form more than 10 per cent of the cover of the technical reserves of an insurance company or of the assets representative of the liabilities of a private pension fund

iv) *securities not traded on a regulated market negotiable within a period not* exceeding *3 months issued by financial institutions headquartered within the EC if these assets are to form more than 20 per cent of the cover of the technical reserves of an insurance company or of the assets representative of the liabilities of a private pension fund.*

List B, V/D1

Operations on money markets:

– Purchase of money market securities abroad by residents.

Remark: the reservation applies to:

i) *money market securities, not traded on a regulated foreign financial market, negotiable within a period exceeding 3 months, excepting securities issued by financial institutions headquartered in the EC, if these assets are to form part of the cover of the technical reserves of an insurance company or of the assets representative of the liabilities of a private pension fund;*

ii) *money market securities, not traded on a regulated foreign financial market, issued by financial institutions headquartered within the EC, if these assets are to form more than 20 per cent of the cover of the technical reserves of an insurance company or of the assets representative of the liabilities of a private pension fund;*

iii) *money market securities, not traded on a regulated market, negotiable within a period not exceeding 3 months, excepting securities issued by financial institutions headquartered in the EC, if these assets are to form more than 10 per cent of the cover of the technical reserves of an insurance company or of the assets representative of the liabilities of a private pension fund;*

iv) *money market securities, not traded on a regulated market, negotiable within a period not exceeding 3 months, issued by financial institutions headquartered within the EC if these assets are to form more than 20 per cent of the cover of the technical reserves of an insurance company or of the assets representative of the liabilities of a private pension fund.*

List B, VI/D1 — Other operations in negotiable instruments and non-securitised claims:

- Purchase abroad by residents.

  Remark: the reservation applies to:

  i) *purchase of or swap operations in instruments and claims, not traded on a regulated foreign financial market, negotiable within a period exceeding 3 months, excepting liabilities of financial institutions headquartered in the EC, if these assets are to form part of the cover of the technical reserves of an insurance company or of the assets representative of the liabilities of a private pension fund;*

  ii) *purchase of or swap operations in instruments and claims, not traded on a regulated foreign financial market, negotiable within a period exceeding 3 months, issued by financial institutions headquartered within the EC, if these assets are to form more than 20 per cent of the cover of the technical reserves of an insurance company or of the assets representative of the liabilities of a private pension fund;*

  iii) *purchase of or swap operations in instruments and claims, not traded on a regulated foreign financial market, negotiable within 3 months, excepting liabilities of financial institutions headquartered within the EC, if these assets are to form more than 10 per cent of the cover of the technical reserves of an insurance company or of the assets representative of the liabilities of a private pension fund;*

  iv) *purchase of or swap operations in instruments and claims, not traded on a regulated foreign financial market, issued by financial institutions headquartered within the EC, if these assets are to form more than 20 per cent of the cover of the technical reserves of an insurance company or of the assets representative of the liabilities of a private pension fund.*

List A, VII/D1 — Operations in collective investment securities:

- Purchase abroad by residents.

  Remark: the reservation applies to securities issued by collective investment funds not regulated by EC authorities if these assets are to form more than 10 per cent of the cover of the technical reserves of an insurance company or of the assets representative of the liabilities of a private pension fund.

| List B, | Financial credits and loans: |
| IX/B | – Credits and loans granted by residents to non-residents. |

Remark: the reservation applies to:

i) *credits and loans granted to non-resident borrowers, other than financial institutions headquartered in the EC, with a residual maturity exceeding 3 months if these assets are to form more than 10 per cent of the cover of the technical reserves of an insurance company or of the assets representative of the liabilities of a private pension fund.*

ii) *credits and loans granted to non-resident financial institutions headquartered in the EC, with a residual maturity exceeding 3 months if these assets are to form more than 20 per cent of the cover of the technical reserves of an insurance company or of the assets representative of the liabilities of a private pension fund.*

List B,	Operation of deposit accounts:
XI/B1,	
B2	– By residents in domestic currency with non-resident institutions.
	– By residents in foreign currency with non-resident institutions.

Remark: the reservation applies to deposits held with financial institutions not supervised by the authorities of an EC country if these deposits are to form part of the cover of the technical reserves of an insurance company or of the assets representative of the liabilities of a private pension fund.

CANADA

General remark: The Canadian authorities undertake to carry out the provisions of the Code to the fullest extent compatible with the constitutional system of Canada in that the latter provides that individual provinces may have jurisdiction to act with respect to certain matters under the purview of the Code. In particular, the authorities undertake to make every effort to ensure that measures for the liberalisation of capital movements are applied in their provinces; they will notify the Organisation of any measure taken by a province that would affect capital movements and, if necessary, they will bring to the attention of the provincial authorities any concerns expressed in this respect by a country subscribing to the Code.

*List A, Direct investment:

I/A
- In the country concerned by non-residents.

   Remark: The reservation applies only to:

   i) *a review requirement applying to large acquisitions of Canadian businesses (direct acquisition involving more than $5 million assets, indirect acquisition involving more than $50 million assets, indirect acquisition involving $5 to $50 million assets representing more than 50 per cent total international transactions assets);*

   ii) *activities related to Canada's cultural heritage or national identity (in particular, those areas involving the publication, distribution and sale of books, magazines and newspapers; films; music; video and audio recordings; and radio and television);*

   iii) *banking and financial services;*

   iv) *insurance;*

   v) *air transport;*

   vi) *maritime transport;*

   vii) *telecommunications;*

   viii) *energy;*

   ix) *fish harvesting.*

List B, III/A1, B1	Operations in real estate:
	- In the country concerned by non-residents.
	- Building or purchase abroad by residents.

Remark: the reservation applies to the acquisition by a private pension fund of real estate abroad which would cause the sum of its assets localised outside Canada to exceed 30 per cent of its total assets.

List A, IV/C1, DI	Operations in securities on capital markets:
	– Purchase in the country concerned by non-residents.

Remark: The reservation applies only to the purchase of shares and other securities of a participating nature which may be affected by laws on inward direct investment and establishment.

– Purchase abroad by residents.

Remark: the reservation applies to the acquisition by a private pension fund of securities issued by non-residents on a foreign financial market which would cause the sum of its assets localised outside Canada to exceed 30 per cent of its total assets.

List B, V/D1	Operations on money markets:
	– Purchase of money market securities abroad by residents.

Remark: the reservation applies to the acquisition by a private pension fund of securities issued by non-residents on a foreign financial market which would cause the sum of its assets localised outside Canada to exceed 30 per cent of its total assets.

List B, VI/D1	Other operations in negotiable instruments and non-securitised claims:
	– Purchase abroad by residents.

Remark: the reservation applies to purchase of or swap operations by a private pension fund in instruments and claims on a foreign financial market which would cause the sum of its assets localised outside Canada to exceed 30 per cent of its total assets.

List A, VII/D1	Operations in collective investment securities:
	– Purchase abroad by residents.

Remark: the reservation applies to purchase by a private pension fund of securities issued on a foreign financial market which would cause the sum of its assets localised outside Canada to exceed 30 per cent of its total assets.

List B, IX/B	Financial credits and loans:
	– Credits and loans granted by residents to non-residents.

Remark: the reservation applies to credits and loans granted to non-resident borrowers by a private pension fund which would cause the sum of its assets localised outside Canada to exceed 30 per cent of its total assets.

List B, XI/B1, B2	Operation of deposit accounts:
	- By residents in domestic currency with non-resident institutions.
	- By residents in foreign currency with non-resident institutions.

Remark: the reservation applies to deposits of funds with non-resident financial institutions by a private pension fund which would cause the sum of its assets localised outside Canada to exceed 30 per cent of its total assets.

List A, Direct investment:

I/A
  – In the country concerned by non-residents.

Remark: The reservation applies to:

i) *the purchase of real estate comprising the agricultural land fund and forests by branches of non-resident enterprises;*

ii) *the operation of a branch as a "mortgage bank" to the extent that a "mortgage bank" is defined under Czech law as an institution authorised to issue mortgage securities on domestic markets, which is reserved to financial institutions incorporated under domestic law;*

iii) *air transport;*

iv) *operation of lotteries and similar games:*

Remark: This reservation does not apply to

a) *betting games in casinos for which an authorisation may be granted to legal persons established in the Czech Republic;*

b) *consumer lotteries in which the prize may be only in-kind fulfilment, services or goods, products, etc, provided that the total value of the in-kind prizes for one calendar year does not exceed the sum of 200 000 Czech crowns and the value of one prize does not exceed the sum of 20 000 Czech crowns.*

List B, Operations in real estate:

III/A1,
B1
  - Building or purchase in the country concerned by non-residents.

  - Building or purchase abroad by residents.

Remark: The reservation applies to:

i) *the acquisition of real estate abroad by a private pension fund;*

ii) *the acquisition of real estate abroad by an insurance company if these assets are to form part of the cover of its technical reserves.*

List A, IV/B1, C1, DI	Operations in securities on capital markets:

– Issue through placing or public sale of foreign securities on the domestic capital market.

Remark: The reservation applies only to mortgage securities.

– Purchase in the country concerned by non-residents.

Remark: The reservation applies only to the purchase of shares and other securities of a participating nature which may be affected by regulations on inward direct investment and establishment in air transport.

– Purchase abroad by residents.

Remark: the reservation only applies to:

i) the purchase by a private pension fund of securities other than those issued by governments and central banks of OECD Member Countries on a foreign market;

ii) the purchase by an insurance company of securities other than those issued by governments and central banks of OECD countries if these assets are to form 75 per cent or less of the cover of its technical reserves and by EIB, EBRD and IBRD if these assets are to form 50 per cent or less of the cover of its technical reserves;

iii) the purchase by an insurance company of securities not traded on a regulated OECD market if these assets are to form 10 per cent or less of the cover of its technical reserves.

List B, V/B1, D1	Operations on money markets:

– Issue through placing or public sale of foreign securities and other instruments on the domestic money market.

Remark: The reservation applies only to mortgage securities.

– Purchase of money market securities abroad by residents.

Remark: the reservation only applies to:

i) the purchase by a private pension fund of securities other than those issued by governments and central banks of OECD Member Countries on a foreign financial market;

ii) *the purchase by an insurance company of securities other than those issued by governments and central banks of OECD member countries if these assets are to form 75 per cent or less of the cover of its technical reserves and by EIB, EBRD and IBRD if these assets are to form 50 per cent or less of the cover of its technical reserves;*

iii) *the purchase by an insurance company of securities not traded on a regulated OECD market if these assets are to form 10 per cent or less of the cover of its technical reserves.*

List B, VI/D1 Other operations in negotiable instruments and non-securitised claims:

  – Purchase abroad by residents.

Remark: the reservation only applies to:

i) *purchase of or swap operations by a private pension fund in instruments and claims on a foreign financial market other than those issued by or contracted with governments and central banks of OECD Member countries;*

ii) *purchase of or swap operations by an insurance company in instruments and claims on a foreign financial market other than derivatives publicly traded on an OECD market if these assets are to form 5 per cent or less of the cover of its technical reserves.*

List A, VII/D1 Operations in collective investment securities:

  – Purchase abroad by residents.

Remark: the reservation only applies to:

i) *purchase by a private pension fund of securities issued on a foreign market;*

ii) *purchase by an insurance company of securities not traded on a regulated OECD market if these assets are to form part of the cover of its technical reserves.*

List B, IX/B Financial credits and loans:

  – Credits and loans granted by residents to non-residents.

Remark: the reservation only applies to:

i) *credits and loans granted to non-resident borrowers other than governments and central banks of OECD member countries by a private pension fund;*

ii) *credits and loans granted to non-resident borrowers by an insurance company if these assets are to form part of the cover of its technical reserves.*

List B, XI/B1, B2

Operation of deposit accounts:

– By residents in domestic currency with non-resident institutions.

– By residents in foreign currency with non-resident institutions.

Remark: the reservation only applies to the deposit of funds with non-resident institutions by a private pension fund or by an insurance company if these assets are to form part of the cover of its technical reserves.

DENMARK

*List A,   Direct investment:

I/A
   – In the country concerned by non-residents.

   Remark: The reservation applies only to:

   i)   ownership of Danish flag vessels by non-EC residents except through an enterprise incorporated in Denmark;

   ii)   ownership by non-EC residents of one-third or more of a business engaged in commercial fishing;

   iii)   ownership of an air transport license, which is reserved to EC residents.

   iv)   investment in accountancy services by non-EC residents and in legal services by non-residents.

List B,   Operations in real estate:

III/A1
   – In the country concerned by non-residents.

   Remark: The reservation does not apply to the acquisition of real estate by:

   i)   persons who have formerly been residents of Denmark for at least five years;

   ii)   EC nationals working in Denmark and EC-based companies operating in Denmark, for residential or business purposes;

   iii)   non-EC nationals who are either in possession of a valid residence permit or are entitled to stay in Denmark without such a permit, for residential or active business purposes.

FINLAND[1]

*List A, Direct investment:

I/A
- In the country concerned by non-residents.

    Remark: The reservation applies only to:

    i)   *establishment of branches of foreign companies, unless an authorisation is granted;*

    ii)   *investment in an enterprise engaged in activities involving nuclear energy or nuclear matter;*

    iii)   *investment in enterprises operating an airline, unless otherwise implied by international agreements to which Finland is a party;*

    iv)   *ownership of Finnish flag vessels, including fishing vessels, except through an enterprise incorporated in Finland;*

    v)   *investment in real estate in the Aaland Islands;*

    vi)   *legal services: EC nationality and residency requirement for investment in a corporation or partnership carrying out the activities "asianajaja" or "advokat";*

    vii)   *investment in auditing companies by non-EC residents.*

List B, Operations in real estate:

III/A1, B1
- In the country concerned by non-residents.

    Remark: The reservation applies only to the acquisition of real estate in the Aaland Islands.

- Building or purchase abroad by residents.

---

1   The provisions of the Revised Capital Movements Code concerning items IV-XII, XV and XVI do not apply for the time being to the Aaland Islands which accordingly have neither rights nor obligations under these items.

Remark: the reservation applies to the acquisition of real estate localised outside the EC, if these assets are to form more than 5 per cent of the cover of the technical reserves of an insurance company or of the assets representative of the liabilities of a private pension fund administering statutory pension schemes.

List A, IV/C1, DI

Operations in securities on capital markets:

– Purchase in the country concerned by non-residents.

Remark: The reservation applies only to the purchase of shares and other securities of a participating nature which may be affected by laws on inward direct investment and establishment.

– Purchase abroad by residents.

Remark: the reservation applies to the purchase of securities issued by non-EC residents if these assets are to form *more than 5 per cent of the cover of the technical reserves of an insurance company or of the assets representative of the liabilities of a private pension fund administering statutory pension schemes.*

List B, V/D1

Operations on money markets:

– Purchase of money market securities abroad by residents.

Remark: the reservation applies to the purchase of securities issued by non-EC residents if these assets are to form more than 5 per cent of the cover of the technical reserves of an insurance company or of the assets representative of the liabilities of a private pension fund administering statutory pension schemes.

List B, VI/D1

Other operations in negotiable instruments and non-securitised claims:

– Purchase abroad by residents.

Remark: the reservation applies to purchase of or swap operations in instruments and claims issued by or contracted with non-EC residents if these assets are to form more than 5 per cent of the cover of the technical reserves of an insurance company or of the assets representative of the liabilities of a private pension fund administering statutory pension schemes.

List A, VII/D1

Operations in collective investment securities:

– Purchase abroad by residents.

Remark: the reservation applies to the purchase of securities issued by non-EC residents if these assets are to form more *than 5 per cent of the cover of the technical reserves of an insurance company or of the assets representative of the liabilities of a private pension fund administering statutory pension schemes.*

List B,
IX/B

Financial credits and loans:

   –   Credits and loans granted by residents to non-residents.

Remark: the reservation applies to credits and loans granted to non-EC residents, if these assets are to form more than 5 per cent of the cover of the technical *reserves of an insurance company or of the assets representative of the liabilities of a private pension fund administering statutory pension schemes.*

List B,
XI/B1,
B2

Operation of deposit accounts:

   -   By residents in domestic currency with non-resident institutions.

   -   By residents in foreign currency with non-resident institutions.

Remark: the reservation applies to deposits of funds with financial institutions regulated by non-EC authorities, if these assets are to form more than 5 per cent of the cover of the technical reserves of an insurance company or of the assets representative of the liabilities of a private pension fund administering statutory pension schemes.

FRANCE

*List A, Direct investment:
I/A
— In the country concerned by non-residents.

Remark: The reservation applies only to:

i) *the establishment of an agricultural enterprise by nationals of countries that are not members of the EC and the acquisition of vineyards;*

ii) *investment in air transport, unless at least 50 per cent of the equity capital is held by nationals of the EC and subject to the provisions of duly approved international agreements that imply otherwise; moreover, the State has full powers regarding domestic air transport with respect to investment not originating in the EC;*

iii) *ownership after acquisition of more than 50 per cent of a French flag vessel, unless the vessel concerned is entirely owned by enterprises having their principal office in France. Moreover, nationals of countries that are not members of the EC may not engage in cabotage.*

List A, Operations in securities on capital markets:
IV/C1
- Purchase in the country concerned by non-residents.

Remark: The reservation applies only to the purchase by non-EC residents of securities not quoted on a recognised securities market which may be affected by laws on inward direct investment and establishment.

List B, Operations on money markets:
V/B1
— Issue through placing or public sale of foreign securities and other instruments on the domestic money market.

Remark: The reservation applies only to the issue of certificates of deposit by non-resident banks.

List A, VII/B1, B2

Operations in collective investment securities:

– Issue through placing or public sale of foreign collective investment securities on the domestic securities market.

Remark: The reservation does not apply to collective investment securities that are of EC origin and comply with EC Directive 85/611/EC.

– Introduction of foreign collective investment securities on a recognised domestic securities market.

Remark: The reservation does not apply to collective investment securities that are of EC origin and comply with EC Directive 85/611/EC.

GERMANY

*List A,   Direct investment:
I/A
–   In the country concerned by non-residents.

   Remark: The reservation applies only to:

   i)   the role of depository bank for investment funds of capital investment companies, which is not permitted to branches of non-resident financial institutions having their head office outside the EC;

   ii)   investment in an air transport enterprise exceeding 25 per cent of the capital;

   iii) acquisition of a German flag vessel, except through an enterprise incorporated in Germany;

   iv)   investment in the broadcasting (radio and television) sector except through a subsidiary incorporated in a German Land, as required for both residents and non-residents.

List B,   Operations in real estate:
III/B1
–   Building or purchase abroad by residents.

   Remark: The reservation applies to the acquisition of real estate outside the EC by insurance companies and "Pensionskassen" if the assets in question are to form more than 5 per cent of their premium reserve stock ("Deckungsstock") or more than 20 per cent of their other restricted assets.

List A,   Operations in securities on capital markets:
IV/D1
–   Purchase abroad by residents.

   Remark: The reservation applies to:

   i)   the purchase by insurance companies and "Pensionskassen" of securities issued by non-EC residents if these assets are to form more than 5 per cent of their premium reserve stock ("Deckungsstock") or more than 20 per cent of their other restricted assets;

ii)   *the purchase by insurance companies and "Pensionskassen"*
      of shares not quoted on an EC stock exchange if these assets
      are to form more than 6 per cent of their premium reserve
      stock ("Deckungsstock") or more than 20 per cent of their
      other restricted assets.

List B,   Operations on money markets:
V/D1
      –   Purchase of money market securities abroad by residents.

      Remark: The reservation applies to the purchase by insurance
      companies and "Pensionskassen" of money market instruments
      with maturities exceeding twelve months issued by non-EC
      residents if these assets are to form more than 5 per cent of their
      premium reserve stock ("Deckungsstock") or more than 20 per
      cent of their other restricted assets.

List B,   Other operations in negotiable instruments and non-securitised
VI/D1   claims:

      –   Purchase abroad by residents.

      Remark: The reservation applies to the purchase by insurance
      companies and "Pensionskassen" of securities issued by non-EC
      residents if these assets are to form more than 5 per cent of their
      premium reserve stock ("Deckungsstock") or more than 20 per
      cent of their other restricted assets.

List A,   Operations in collective investment securities:
VII/D1
      –   Purchase abroad by residents.

      Remark: The reservation applies to the purchase by insurance
      companies and "Pensionskassen" of collective investment
      securities issued by non-EC residents if these assets are to form
      more than 5 per cent of their premium reserve stock
      ("Deckungsstock") or more than 20 per cent of their other
      restricted assets.

List B,   Financial credits and loans:
IX/B
      –   Credits and loans granted by residents to non-residents.

      Remark: The reservation applies to the granting by insurance
      companies and "Pensionskassen" of credits to non-EC residents if
      these assets are to form more than 5 per cent of their premium
      reserve stock ("Deckungsstock") or more than 20 per cent of their
      other restricted assets.

List B,	Operation of deposit accounts:
XI/B1, B2	- By residents in domestic currency with non-resident institutions.
	- By residents in foreign currency with non-resident institutions.

Remark: The reservation applies to deposits of funds by insurance companies and "Pensionskassen" with financial institutions regulated by non-EC authorities if these assets are to form more than 5 per cent of their premium reserve stock ("Deckungsstock") or more than 20 per cent of their other restricted assets.

GREECE

*List A,   Direct investment:

I/A
–   In the country concerned by non-residents.

Remark: The reservation applies only to non-EC investors as follows:

i)   acquisition of real estate in border regions;

ii)   investment in the mining sector unless concession in mineral rights are granted;

iii)   establishment of a representative office or a branch of a foreign bank, unless an authorisation is granted;

iv)   ownership of more than 49 per cent of the capital of an Greek airline company, cabotage is reserved to Greek airline companies;

v)   ownership of more than 49 per cent of the capital of a Greek flag vessel for maritime transport or fishing purposes;

vi)   ownership of more than 25 per cent of the capital of a television (including cable television) company and 49 per cent of the capital of a radio broadcasting company;

vii)   investment by non-EC nationals in the accountancy, legal, engineering and architectural sector.

List B,   Operations in real estate:

III/A1,
B1
–   Building or purchase by non-residents.

Remark: The reservation applies only to the acquisition of real estate in border regions by non-EC residents.

–   Building or purchase abroad by residents.

Remark: the reservation applies to:

i)   the acquisition of real estate abroad if the asset in question is to form more than one third of the guarantee funds of a local branch of a non-EC insurance company established in Greece;

ii) the acquisition of real estate outside the EC if the asset in question is to form part of the cover of the prescribed solvency margin for the local branch of a non-EC insurance company established in Greece or is to form part of the cover of technical reserves of resident insurance companies.

List A, IV/C1, D1

Operations in securities on capital markets:

– Purchase in the country concerned by non-residents.

Remark: The reservation applies only to the purchase of shares and other securities of a participation nature in the broadcasting and maritime sectors which may be affected by the laws on inward direct investment and establishment.

– Purchase abroad by residents.

Remark: the reservation applies to the purchase of securities issued by non-EC residents if these assets are to form part of the technical reserves of an insurance *company.*

List B, V/D1

Operations on money markets:

– Purchase of money market securities abroad by residents.

Remark: the reservation applies to the acquisition of securities issued by non-EC residents if these assets are to form part of the technical reserves of an insurance company.

List B, VI/D1

Other operations in negotiable instruments and non-securitised claims:

– Purchase abroad by residents.

Remark: the reservation applies *to purchase of or swap operations in instruments and claims issued by or contracted with non-EC residents if these assets are to form part of the technical reserves of an insurance company.*

List A, VII/D1

Operations in collective investment securities:

– Purchase abroad by residents.

Remark: the reservation applies to the purchase of securities issued by non-EC residents if these assets are to form part of the technical reserves of an insurance company.

List B, IX/B	Financial credits and loans:

– Credits and loans granted by residents to non-residents.

Remark: the reservation applies to credits and loans granted to non-EC residents, if these assets are to form part of the technical reserves of an insurance company.

List B, XI/B1, B2	Operation of deposit accounts:

- By residents in domestic currency with non-resident institutions.

- By residents in foreign currency with non-resident institutions.

Remark: the reservation applies to deposits of funds with financial institutions regulated by non-EC authorities, if these assets are to form part of the technical reserves of an insurance company.

HUNGARY

List A, Direct investment:
I/A
   – In the country concerned by non-residents.

     Remark: The reservation applies only to:

    i)   *Acquisition of a license for domestic air transport, which is reserved to majority-owned and -controlled Hungarian enterprises;*

    ii) *Acquisition of a shipping license to operate in international waters, which is reserved to firms majority-owned or controlled by Hungarians;*

    iii) *The provision of asset management services by branches of non-resident investors to domestic compulsory private pension funds.*

List B, Operations in real estate:
III/A1,
B1   – In the country concerned by non-residents.

   - Building or purchase abroad by residents.

     Remark: the reservation applies to the acquisition of real *estate abroad:*

    i)   *if such assets are to form the security capital and technical reserves of an insurance company;*

    ii) *by a voluntary pension fund.*

List A, Operations in securities on capital markets:
IV/C1,
D1   – Purchase in the country concerned by non-residents.

     Remark: The reservation applies only to the purchase of shares and other securities of participating nature which may be affected by regulations on inward direct investment and establishment in air transport and in companies licensed to operate in international waters.

– Purchase abroad by residents.

Remark: The reservation applies to the purchase of:

i) *securities issued by non-residents on a foreign market if such assets are to form the mathematical reserves of an insurance company;*

ii) *debt securities issued by non-resident credit institutions which would exceed 20 per cent of the assets constituting the security capital of an insurance company;*

iii) *securities issued by non-residents by a mandatory pension fund which would exceed 30 per cent of its total assets;*

iv) *securities issued by non-residents on a foreign market by a voluntary pension fund which would cause the sum of its assets invested outside Hungary to exceed 30 per cent of its total assets.*

List B, V/D1
Operations on money markets:

– Purchase of money market securities abroad by residents.

Remark: The reservation applies to the purchase of:

i) *securities issued by non-residents on a foreign market if such assets are to form the mathematical reserves of an insurance company;*

ii) *securities issued by non-residents by a mandatory pension fund which would exceed 30 per cent of its total assets;*

iii) *securities issued by non-residents on a foreign market by a voluntary pension fund which would cause the sum of its assets invested outside Hungary to exceed 30 per cent of its total assets.*

List A, VII/D1
Operations in collective investment securities:

– Purchase abroad by residents.

Remark: The reservation applies to the purchase of:

i) *securities issued by non-residents on a foreign market if such assets are to form the mathematical reserves of an insurance company;*

ii) *securities issued by non-residents by a mandatory pension fund which would exceed 30 per cent of its total assets;*

iii)   *securities issued by non-residents on a foreign market by a voluntary pension fund which would cause the sum of its assets invested   outside Hungary to exceed 30 per cent of its total assets.*

List B, IX/B   Financial credits and loans:

–   Credits and loans granted by residents to non-residents.

Remark: The reservation applies to credits and loans granted to non-residents if such asset is a mortgage loan based on real estate collateral situated outside Hungary and is to form part of the security capital of an insurance company.

List B, XI/B1, B2   Operation of deposit accounts:

-   By residents in domestic currency with non-resident institutions.

-   By residents in foreign currency with non-resident institutions.

Remark: The reservation applies to:

i)   *deposits of funds with non-resident financial institutions by an insurance company if such assets are to form part of its mathematical reserves;*

ii)   *deposits of funds on a current account   with non-resident financial institutions by an insurance company if such assets are to form part of its security capital and technical reserves.*

List B, XII/B1   Operations in foreign exchange:

-   Purchase of foreign currency with domestic currency abroad by residents.

Remark: the reservation applies to the purchase of foreign currency with domestic currency if such assets are to form the cover of the mathematical reserves of an insurance company.

ICELAND

*List A,   Direct investment:

I/A
     –   In the country concerned by non-residents.

Remark: The reservation applies only to:

   i)   *investment exceeding ISK 250 million per annum by a single investor, unless an authorisation is granted;*

   ii)   *investment raising above 25 per cent the non-resident share of the total stock of investment in aquaculture, communications, manufacturing other than power intensive industries, trade and services, unless an authorisation is granted;*

   iii) *investment that seriously reduces competition between enterprises in any sector or is otherwise likely to have an undesirable effect on the Icelandic economy;*

   iv) *investment by foreign states or state-owned enterprises, unless an authorisation is granted;*

   v)   *investment in real estate, except for a legal entity which has acquired rights to conduct a business enterprise and provided that the real estate is only accompanied by normal rights to ground and does not include other rights, such as fishing or water exploitation rights;*

   vi) *acquisition of rights to natural resources or energy exploitation, and investment in energy production or distribution;*

   vii) *investment in fishing and primary fish processing (i.e. excluding retail packaging and later stages of preparation of fish products for distribution and consumption);*

   viii) *establishment of subsidiaries of foreign banks, and investment in domestic banks exceeding 25 per cent of share capital;*

   ix) *investment in an air transport company exceeding 49 per cent of share capital;*

   x)   *ownership of Icelandic flag vessels, except through an enterprise incorporated in Iceland.*

List B, III/A1 Operations in real estate:

– In the country concerned by non-residents.

Remark: The reservation does not apply to the building or purchase of real estate where:

i)   in the case of limited-liability companies non-resident ownership does not exceed 1/5 of the total equity and Icelandic citizens hold a majority of the total voting power at shareholders' meetings;

ii)   an authorisation is granted.

List A, IV/C1 Operations in securities on capital markets:

– Purchase in the country concerned by non-residents.

Remark: The reservation applies only to the purchase of shares or other securities of a participating nature which may be affected by laws on inward direct investment and establishment.

IRELAND

*List A,
I/A

Direct investment:

– In the country concerned by non-residents.

Remark: The reservation applies only to:

i) *investment in air transport by non-EC States or nationals of non-EC States;*

ii) *acquisition by non-EC nationals of land for agricultural purposes, unless an authorisation is granted;*

iii) *acquisition of Irish-registered shipping vessels except through an enterprise incorporated in Ireland;*

iv) *acquisition by non-EC nationals of sea fishing vessels registered in Ireland;*

v) *investment by residents of non-EC member countries in flour milling activities.*

List B,
III/A1

Operations in real estate:

– In the country concerned by non-residents.

Remark: The reservation applies only to the acquisition of an interest in rural land for which authorisation is required, other than land not exceeding two hectares in area and acquired for private residential purposes.

*List A, Direct investment:

I/A
– In the country concerned by non-residents.

Remark: The reservation applies only to:

i)   *majority participation or controlling interest in companies that publish daily newspapers and periodicals;*

ii)   *licence granted to audio-visual communications enterprises having their headquarters in a non-EC member country;*

iii) *majority participation by non-EC residents in companies licensed for television and sound-radio broadcasting, and participation by non-EC residents in companies having no legal personality and licensed for television and sound-radio broadcasting;*

iv)   *the purchase by foreigners of aircraft in Italy and foreign ownership exceeding one-third of the share capital of companies possessing such aircraft;*

v)   *the purchase by foreigners other than EC residents of a majority interest in Italian flag vessels or of a controlling interest in ship owning companies having their headquarters in Italy;*

vi)   *the purchase of Italian flag vessels used to fish in Italian territorial waters;*

vii) *the establishment of branches, agencies, etc. of securities investment companies.*

List A, Physical movement of capital assets:

XV/B1,
B2
- Import of means of payment.

Remark: The reservation applies only to the import of gold.

- Export of means of payment.

Remark: The reservation applies only to the export of gold.

JAPAN

*List A,
I/A, B

Direct investment:

– In the country concerned by non-residents.

Remark: The reservation applies only to:

i) *investment in the following sectors:*

a) *primary industry related to agriculture, forestry and fisheries;*

b) *mining;*

c) *oil;*

d) *leather and leather products manufacturing;*

ii) *investment in air transport;*

iii) *investment in maritime transport.*

– Abroad by residents.

Remark: The reservation applies only to investments in an enterprise engaged in fishing regulated by international treaties to which Japan is a party or fishing operations coming under the Japanese Fisheries Law.

List B,
III/B1

Operations in real estate:

– Building or purchase abroad by residents.

Remark: the reservation applies to the acquisition by an insurance company of real estate abroad which would cause the sum of its assets denominated in foreign currency to exceed 30 per cent of its total assets.

List A,
IV/ D1

Operations in securities on capital markets:

– Purchase abroad by residents.

Remark: the reservation applies to the purchase by an insurance company of securities issued on a foreign financial market or in foreign currency on the domestic market which would cause the sum of its assets denominated in foreign currency to exceed 30 per cent of its total assets.

81

List B, V/C2, D1	Operations on money markets:

- Purchase of money market securities abroad by residents.

   Remark: the reservation applies to the acquisition or repurchase by an insurance company of securities issued on a foreign financial market or in foreign currency on the domestic *market which would cause the sum of its assets denominated in foreign currency to exceed 30 per cent of its total assets.*

List B, VI/D1	Other operations in negotiable instruments and non-securitised claims:

- Purchase abroad by residents.

   Remark: the reservation applies to purchase of or swap operations by an insurance company in instruments and claims denominated in foreign currency on foreign or domestic markets which would cause the sum of its assets denominated *in foreign currency to exceed 30 per cent of its total assets.*

List A, VII/D1	Operations in collective investment securities:

- Purchase abroad by residents.

   Remark: the reservation applies to purchase by an insurance company of securities issued on a foreign financial market or in foreign currency on the domestic market which would *cause the sum of its assets denominated in foreign currency to exceed 30 per cent of its total assets.*

List B, IX/B	Financial credits and loans:

- Credits and loans granted by residents to non-residents.

   Remark: the reservation applies to credits and loans granted to non-resident borrowers by an insurance company or in foreign currency to resident borrowers *which would cause the sum of its assets denominated in foreign currency to exceed 30 per cent of its total assets.*

List B,
XI/B1,
B2

Operation of deposit accounts:

- By residents in domestic currency with non-resident institutions.

- By residents in foreign currency with non-resident institutions.

  Remark: the reservation applies to deposits of funds with non-resident financial *institutions or foreign-currency denominated funds with resident financial institutions by an insurance company which would cause the sum of its assets denominated in foreign currency to exceed 30 per cent of its total assets.*

KOREA

List A,
I/A, B

Direct investment:

– In the country concerned by non-residents.

Remark: The reservation applies only to:

i) *investment in primary sectors, as follows:*

a) *the growing of rice and barley;*

b) *cattle husbandry and the wholesale selling of meat except if foreign investors hold less than 50 per cent of the share capital;*

c) *the Korea Tobacco & Ginseng Corporation to the extent that aggregate foreign ownership is limited to 49 per cent of its total capital;*

d) *fishing in internal waters, the territorial sea and the Exclusive Economic Zone (EEZ) if foreign investors hold 50 per cent or more of the share capital;*

e) *nuclear power generation; electric power transmission, electric power distribution and supply via state enterprises if foreign investors hold 50 per cent or more of the share capital or a foreign investor would become the single largest shareholder;*

ii) *establishment of financial institutions, as follows:*

a) *branches of mutual savings and finance companies, short-term investment and finance companies, credit information companies and merchant banks;*

b) *subsidiaries or joint ventures providing credit information services, when foreign investors, other than foreign financial institutions, own 50 percent or more of the companies' shares; as well as acquisitions bringing foreign ownership by investors other than foreign financial institutions at or above 50 percent of the share capital of such a company.*

iii) *investment in the transport sector, as follows:*

   a) *airline companies if foreign investors hold 50 per cent or more of the share capital;*

   b) *shipping companies engaged in cabotage, except those transporting passengers and/or cargoes between the ROK and the DPRK if foreign investors hold less than 50 per cent of the share capital;*

iv) *investment in the communications sector, as follows:*

   a) *news agencies if foreign investors hold 25 per cent or more of the share capital;*

   b) *enterprises publishing newspapers if foreign investors hold 30 per cent or more of the share capital;*

   c) *enterprises publishing periodicals if foreign investors hold 50 per cent or more of the share capital;*

   d) *broadcasting companies, except if foreign investors hold 33 per cent or less of the share capital of non-news program providers, in cable TV system operators and in satellite broadcasters and if foreign investors hold 49 per cent or less in cable network operators;*

   e) *facilities-based telecommunications companies, if foreign investors hold more than 49 per cent of the share capital;*

v) *investment in designated resident public-sector utilities in the process of privatisation, in cases where the investment in question would bring individual or aggregate holdings of foreign investors above the respective percentages of a firm's outstanding shares allowed by the relevant laws.*

– Abroad by residents.

Remark: *The reservation applies only to investment by individual entrepreneurs in excess of 30 per cent of their previous accounting year's total sales or more than US$ 1 million, whichever is greater.*

List B,
III/B1

Operations in real estate:

–   Building or purchase abroad by residents.

Remark: The reservation does not apply to the acquisition of:

i)   *residences whose prices do not exceed US$ 0.5 million and do not entail capital transfers from Korea of more than US$ 0.3 million, by resident natural persons who have resided or will reside abroad for at least 2 years for business or official purposes;*

ii) *real estate by resident enterprises for business purposes;*

iii) *real estate by an insurance company which would not cause the sum of its assets denominated in foreign currency to exceed 10 per cent of its total assets.*

List A,
IV/C1,
D1

Operations in securities on capital markets:

–   Purchase in the country concerned by non-residents.

Remark: The reservation applies only to the purchase of listed shares issued by designated resident public-sector utilities in the process of privatisation in cases where the investment in question would bring individual or aggregate holdings of foreign investors above the respective percentages of a firm's outstanding shares allowed by the relevant laws and to the purchase of securities not quoted on a recognised securities market which may be affected by laws on inward direct investment and establishment.

–   Purchase abroad by residents.

Remark: The reservation applies to the purchase by an insurance company of securities issued on a foreign financial market or in foreign currency on the domestic market which would cause the sum of its assets denominated in foreign currency to exceed 10 per cent of its total assets.

List B,
V/A1,
B1, C3,
C4, D1,
D3, D4

Operations on money markets:

– Issue through placing or public sale of domestic securities and other instruments on a foreign money market.

Remark: The reservation does not apply to the issue of securities denominated in foreign currency by authorised resident foreign exchange banks or by resident companies with a debt/equity ratio below the average level of the respective industry which have been rated investment grade by domestic or international credit rating agencies.

– Issue through placing or public sale of foreign securities and other instruments on the domestic money market.

Remark: The reservation does not apply to the issue of securities denominated in foreign currency.

– Lending through other money market instruments in the country concerned by non-residents.

Remark: The reservation does not apply to operations in foreign currency between non-resident banks and authorised resident foreign exchange banks.

– Borrowing through other money market instruments in the country concerned by non-residents.

Remark: The reservation does not apply to operations in foreign currency between non-resident banks and authorised resident foreign exchange banks.

– Purchase of money market securities abroad by residents.

Remark: The reservation only applies to the purchase of securities denominated in domestic currency and to purchase by an insurance company of securities issued on a foreign financial market or in foreign currency on the domestic market which would cause the sum of its assets denominated in foreign currency to exceed 10 per cent of its total assets.

– Lending through other money market instruments abroad by residents.

Remark: The reservation does not apply to lending in foreign currency by authorised resident foreign exchange banks.

–   Borrowing through other money market instruments abroad by residents.

Remark: The reservation does not apply to operations between non-resident banks and authorised resident foreign exchange banks.

List B,
VI/A1,
A2, B1,
B2, C1,
C3, D1,
D2, D3

Other operations in negotiable instruments and non-securitised claims:

-   Issue through placing or public sale of domestic instruments and claims on a foreign financial market.

-   Introduction of domestic instruments and claims on a recognised foreign financial market.

-   Issue through placing or public sale of foreign instruments and claims on a domestic financial market.

-   Introduction of foreign instruments and claims on a recognised domestic financial market.

-   Purchase in the country concerned by non-residents.

Remark: The reservation does not apply to the purchase of stock index futures and options.

–   Exchange for other assets in the country concerned by non-residents.

Remark: The reservation does not apply to transactions where one of the parties is a resident authorised foreign exchange bank.

–   Purchase abroad by residents.

Remark: The reservation does not apply to transactions where a resident authorised foreign exchange bank is a party.

–   Sale abroad by residents.

Remark: The reservation does not apply to transactions to which a resident authorised foreign exchange bank is a party.

–   Exchange for other assets abroad by residents.

Remark: The reservation does not apply to transactions where a resident authorised foreign exchange bank is a party.

List A, VII/B1, D1	Operations in collective investment securities:

List A, VII/B1, D1 — Issue through placing or public sale of foreign collective investment securities on the domestic securities market.

Remark: The reservation does not apply to the issue of collective investment securities by foreign investment trust companies which invest their funds only in foreign securities.

— Purchase abroad by residents.

Remark: The reservation applies to purchase by an insurance company of securities issued on a foreign financial market or in foreign currency on the domestic market which would cause the sum of its assets denominated in foreign currency to exceed 30 per cent of its total assets.

List A, VIII(i)/ A, B — Credits directly linked with international commercial transactions or the rendering of international services, in cases where a resident participates in the underlying commercial or service transaction:

— Credits granted by non-residents to residents.

Remark: The reservation applies to commercial credits, other than trade credits (including deferred payments, instalment payments, export advances, export down payments), with an original maturity of one year or less unless the borrower is an authorised resident foreign exchange bank or a resident company with a debt/equity ratio below the average level of the respective industry which has been rated investment grade by domestic or international credit rating agencies.

Credits granted by residents to non-residents.

Remark: The reservation does not apply to:

i)   credits in the form of deferred receipts or advanced payments;

ii)   other credits:

a) in domestic currency granted by authorised foreign exchange banks and institutional investors, up to 1 billion won per borrower;

b) in foreign currency granted by authorised foreign exchange banks, institutional investors, general trading companies up to US$ 10 million, and other enterprises up to US$ 300 000.

89

List B, VIII(ii)/ B	Credits directly linked with international commercial transactions or the rendering of international services, in cases where no resident participates in the underlying commercial or service transaction:

– Credits granted by residents to non-residents.

Remark: The reservation does not apply to:

i) *credits denominated in foreign currency;*

ii) *credits denominated in domestic currency granted by authorised foreign exchange banks and by institutional investors, up to 1 billion won per borrower.*

List B, IX/A, B	Financial credits and loans:

– Credits and loans granted by non-residents to residents.

Remark: The reservation applies to credits and loans with an original maturity of one year or less granted to non-bank resident companies with a debt/equity ratio above the average level of the respective industry which has not been rated investment grade by domestic or international credit rating agencies.

– Credits and loans granted by residents to non-residents.

Remark: The reservation does not apply to:

i) *credits and loans denominated in foreign currency by authorised resident foreign exchange banks;*

ii) *credits and loans denominated in domestic currency granted by authorised foreign exchange banks and by institutional investors up to 1 billion won per borrower.*

List A, X(ii)/A2	Sureties, guarantees and financial back-up facilities in cases not directly related to international trade, international current invisible operations or international capital movement operations, or where no resident participates in the underlying international operation concerned:

– Sureties and guarantees given by residents in favour of non-residents.

Remark: The reservation applies only to sureties and guarantees denominated in domestic currency;

List B, XI/B1, B2	Operation of deposit accounts:

Operation of deposit accounts:

- By residents in domestic currency with non-resident institutions.

- By residents in foreign currency with non-resident institutions.

  Remark: The reservation does not apply to the operation of deposit accounts by:

  i)   *foreign exchange banks;*

  ii) *institutional investors; except that in the case of an insurance company, the sum of its assets denominated in foreign currency must not exceed 10 per cent of its total assets;*

  iii) *corporate investors for amounts not exceeding US$ 5 million per company;*

  iv) *individual persons, with branches and subsidiaries abroad of Korean foreign exchange banks, up to US$ 50 000 (per person and per year);*

  v)   *residents working abroad.*

List B,
XII/B1,
B2, B3

Operations in foreign exchange:

- Purchase of foreign currency with domestic currency abroad by residents.

- Sale of foreign currency for domestic currency abroad by residents.

- Exchange of foreign currencies abroad by residents.

  Remark: The reservation does not apply to operations by authorised foreign exchange banks or spot operations.

List A,
XV/B2

Physical movements of capital assets

- Export of means of payments.

  Remark: The reservation applies only to the export of domestic means of payments in excess of the equivalent of US$ 10 000.

List B, III/B1	Operations in real estate:

    – Building or purchase abroad by residents.

Remark: the reservation applies to the acquisition of real estate situated outside the EC if the assets in question are to form part of the cover of the technical provisions of an insurance company or of a private pension fund.

List A, IV/D1	Operations in securities on capital markets:

    – Purchase abroad by residents.

Remark: the reservation applies to the purchase of securities issued by non-EC residents if the assets in question are to form more than 5 per cent of the cover of the technical provisions of an insurance company or of a private pension fund.

List B, V/D1	Operations on money markets:

    – Purchase of money market securities abroad by residents.

Remark: the reservation applies to the purchase of securities issued by non-EC residents if the assets in question are to form more than 5 per cent of the cover of the technical provisions of an insurance company or of a private pension fund.

List B, VI/D1	Other operations in negotiable instruments and non-securitised claims:

    – Purchase abroad by residents.

Remark: the reservation applies to purchase of or swap operations in instruments and claims issued by non-EC residents if the assets in question are to form more than 5 per cent of the cover of the technical provisions of an insurance company or of a private pension fund.

List A, VII/D1	Operations in collective investment securities:
	– Purchase abroad by residents.

Remark: the reservation applies to the purchase of securities issued by non-EC residents if the assets in question are to form more than 5 per cent of the cover of the technical provisions of an insurance company or of a private pension fund.

List B, IX/B	Financial credits and loans:
	– Credits and loans granted by residents to non-residents.

Remark: the reservation applies to credits and loans granted to non-resident borrowers, if these assets are to form part of the cover of the technical provisions of an insurance company or of a private pension fund.

List B, XI/B1, B2	Operation of deposit accounts:
	- By residents in domestic currency with non-resident institutions.
	- By residents in foreign currency with non-resident institutions.

Remark: the reservation applies to deposits held with financial institutions established outside the EC if these assets are to form part of the technical provisions of an insurance company or of a private pension fund.

MEXICO

List A,
I/A

Direct investment:

– In the country concerned by non-residents.

Remark: The reservation applies only to:

i) *acquisitions exceeding a total of 49 per cent of the equity of a Mexican company, which are subject to review if the total value of the assets of that company exceeds US$ 50 million; this value will be raised to US$ 75 million on 1 January 2000 and US$ 150 million on 1 January 2003.*

ii) *acquisition of land used for agriculture, livestock or forestry purposes; however "T" shares which represent the value of such land may be purchased up to a total of 49 per cent of the value of the land.*

iii) *investment in:*

a) *retail trade in gasoline and distribution of liquefied petroleum gas.*

b) *supply of fuels and lubricants for ships, aircraft and railroad equipment exceeding a total of 49 per cent of equity.*

c) *construction of oil pipelines and other derivative products and oil and gas drilling exceeding a total of 49 per cent of equity, unless an authorisation is granted.*

iv) *investment exceeding a total of 49 per cent in fishing, other than aquaculture, in coastal and fresh waters or in the Exclusive Economic Zone.*

v) *investment in air, maritime and ground transport and related services including cabotage and port services, except:*

a) *participation up to a total of 25 per cent of equity in national air transport, specialised air services and aerotaxi; up to a total of 49 per cent in the administration of air terminals, and above 49 per cent provided an authorisation is granted;*

b) *participation up to a total of 49 per cent of equity in interior navigation and coastal sailing, except tourist cruises and the exploitation of dredges and other naval devices for ports; in integral port administration and port pilot services for interior navigation; and in foreign commerce shipping and port services for interior navigation where participation may be authorised up to 100 per cent;*

c) *railroad related services; and participation up to 49 per cent in the capital stock of a railway concessionaire enterprise (full ownership may be authorised); and*

d) *participation up to 49 per cent of equity in international ground transport of passengers, tourism and loading within Mexico and the administration of bus stations for passengers and auxiliary activities.[1]*

vi) *investment in radio and television broadcasting; investment exceeding a total of 49 per cent of equity in cable television, satellite communications, basic telephone services, newspapers for national distribution; and investment in cellular telephony where participation may be authorised up to 100 per cent.*

vii) *investment by a foreign government or state enterprise in any kind of communications or transports activities or direct or indirect investment by a foreign government or state enterprise, or direct or indirect investment in financial institutions, except for commercial banks, financial holding companies, securities specialists and securities firms where the restriction applies only to investment by entities that exercise governmental authority functions.*

viii) *in the Restricted Zone, acquisition of real estate by branches established in the country by non-resident enterprises and investment in residential real estate by enterprises with foreign participation incorporated in the country.*

---

1. Non-resident investors will be allowed to participate in these sectors up to a total of 51 per cent of equity as of 1 January 2001 and up to 100 per cent as of 1 January 2004.

ix) *investment aircraft building, assembly or repair, in shipbuilding and ship repairs, or in any activity requiring a concession other than railways, except through an enterprise incorporated in Mexico.*

x) *investment by foreign nationals in legal services[1] and private education services exceeding 49 per cent of equity, unless an authorisation is granted;*

xi) *investment in financial institutions, except under the following conditions:*

  a) *ownership up to a total of 49 per cent of the paid-in capital in insurance companies, financial leasing companies, factoring companies, general deposit warehouses, bonding companies and foreign exchange firms; and up to 49 per cent of the capital stock of limited scope financial institutions, securities advisory companies and managing companies of investment companies;*

  b) *ownership of up to 49 per cent of the fixed stock of investment companies;*

  c) *ownership of up to a total of 100 per cent of the common stock in credit information institutions and securities rating agencies;*

  d) *ownership of at least 51 per cent of the common stock in a subsidiary of the following type: bonding companies, general deposit warehouses, foreign exchange firms, pension funds and managing companies and securities specialists, by non-resident financial institutions of the same general type of activities;*

---

1. A professional license in law is required to be a public notary or a commercial public notary. Only a Mexican national by birth may be licensed as a public notary or a commercial public notary. Neither a public notary, nor a commercial public notary may have a business affiliation with any person who is not licensed in the same category of public notary.

e) *ownership of at least 51 per cent of the common stock in a subsidiary of managing companies of investment companies, and of the fixed stock of investment companies, by non-resident financial institutions of the same general type of activities.*

f) *ownership of at least 51 per cent of the common stock in a subsidiary of the following type: banks, securities firms, insurance companies, leasing companies, factoring companies and limited scope financial institutions (Sofoles), by non-resident financial institutions of the same general type of activities;*

g) *ownership of at least 51 per cent and up to a total of 100 per cent of the common stock of existing financial institutions;*

h) *if the sum of the authorised capital of commercial banks owned and controlled by investors from OECD countries, measured as a percentage of the aggregate net capital of all commercial banks in Mexico, reaches 25 per cent, Mexico may request consultations with the OECD Member countries on the potential adverse effects arising from the presence of commercial banks of the other OECD Member countries in the Mexican market and the possible need for remedial action, including further temporary limitations on market participation. The consultation shall be completed expeditiously. In considering the potential adverse effects, the OECD Member countries shall take into account:*

1. *the threat that the Mexican payments system may be controlled by non-Mexican persons;*

2. *the effects that foreign commercial banks established in Mexico may have on Mexico's ability to conduct monetary and exchange rate policy effectively; and*

3. *the adequacy of the provisions of the Codes with respect to financial services in protecting the Mexican payments system;*

i) *from 1 January 2000 to 31 December 2003, the Mexican authorities may freeze, only once and for a period of no more than three years, the aggregate market shares of subsidiaries of non-resident banks or securities firms if they exceed 25 per cent of the net capital of the banking sector or 30 per cent of the global capital of the securities business sector, respectively;*

j) *a non-resident financial institution authorised to establish or acquire a bank or a securities firm may also establish a financial holding company, and thereby establish or acquire other types of financial institutions;*

k) *foreign financial institutions other than banks, securities firms, securities specialists and limited scope financial institutions may establish only one institution of the same type;*

l) *subsidiaries of foreign financial institutions may not establish branches, subsidiaries or agencies outside Mexico.*

List B, III/A1, B1

Operations in real estate:

– In the country concerned by non-residents.

Remark: The reservation does not apply to:

i) *The acquisition by foreign non-residents of real estate outside a 100-kilometre strip alongside the Mexican land border and a 50-kilometre strip inland from the Mexican coast, provided the investor agrees to consider himself Mexican and to refrain from invoking the protection of his government regarding the property thus acquired;*

ii) *The acquisition by foreign non-residents of real estate through a real estate trust within the zone defined above.*

– Building or purchase abroad by residents.

Remark: the reservation applies to the acquisition of real estate abroad by an insurance company or by a privately managed pension fund.

List A, IV/A1, A2, B1, C1, D1

Operations in securities on capital markets:

– Issue through placing or public sale of domestic securities on a foreign capital market.

Remark: The reservation applies only to debt securities denominated in domestic currency.

– Introduction of domestic securities on a recognised foreign capital market.

Remark: The reservation applies only to debt securities denominated in domestic currency.

– Issue through placing or public sale of foreign securities on the domestic capital market.

Remark: The reservation applies only to issues of debt securities through public offer.

– Purchase in the country concerned by non-residents.

Remark: The reservation applies to the purchase of shares and other securities of a participating nature which may be affected by the laws on inward direct investment and establishment.

– Purchase abroad by residents.

Remark: The reservation applies to:

i)   the purchase of foreign securities by securities firms on their own account and on the account of their clients;

ii)   the purchase by an insurance company or a privately managed pension fund of securities denominated in foreign currency, with the exceptions of capital market instruments registered in the special section of the National Register of Securities and Intermediaries and of securities issued in foreign currency by the Federal Government or payable abroad by Mexican financial institutions or by foreign financial entities which are affiliates of these. In the case of private pension funds such assets may not exceed 70 per cent of mandatory reserves.

List B, V/A1, A2, B1, D1	Operations on money markets:

– Issue through placing or public sale of domestic securities and other instruments on a foreign money market.

Remark: The reservation applies only to securities and other instruments denominated in domestic currency.

– Introduction of domestic securities and other instruments on a recognised foreign money market.

Remark: The reservation applies only to securities and other instruments denominated in domestic currency.

– Issue through placing or public sale of foreign securities and other instruments on the domestic money market.

Remark: The reservation applies only to issues through public offer.

– Purchase of money market securities abroad by residents.

Remark: the reservation applies to:

i) the purchase of foreign securities by securities firms on their own account and on the account of their clients;

ii) the purchase by an insurance company or a private pension fund of securities denominated in foreign currency, with the exceptions of money market instruments registered in the special section of the National Register of Securities and Intermediaries and of deposits and securities issued in foreign currency by the Federal Government or payable abroad by Mexican financial institutions or by foreign financial entities which are affiliates of these. In the case of private pension funds such assets may not exceed 70 per cent of mandatory reserves.

List B, VI/B1, B2, D1	Other operations in negotiable instruments and non-securitised claims:

– Issue through placing or public sale of foreign instruments and claims on a domestic financial market.

Remark: The reservation applies only to issues through public offer.

- Introduction of foreign instruments and claims on a recognised domestic financial market.

- Purchase abroad by residents.

  Remark: the reservation applies to purchase of or swap operations in instruments and claims on a foreign financial market by an insurance company or a private pension fund.

List A, VII/B1, B2, D1

Operations in collective investment securities:

– Issue through placing or public sale of foreign collective investment securities on the domestic securities market.

  Remark: The reservation applies only to issues through public offer.

- Introduction of foreign collective investment securities on a recognised domestic securities market.

- Purchase abroad by residents.

  Remark: the reservation applies to purchase by an insurance company or a private pension fund of securities denominated in foreign currency with the exceptions of those securities registered in the special section of the National Register of Securities and Intermediaries and of securities issued in foreign currency payable abroad by Mexican financial institutions or by foreign financial entities which are affiliates of these. In the case of private pension funds such assets may not exceed 70 per cent of mandatory reserves.

List B, IX/B

Financial credits and loans:

– Credits and loans granted by residents to non-residents.

  Remark: the reservation applies to credits and loans denominated in foreign currency granted by an insurance company or a private pension fund.

List A, XI/A2

Operation of deposit accounts:

– By non-residents in foreign currency with resident institutions.

  Remark: The reservation applies only to:

  i)   *non-residents other than enterprises having an address in Mexico;*

  ii) *term deposit accounts of non-residents with resident banks*

List B,
XI/B1,
B2

Operation of deposit accounts:

- By residents in domestic currency with non-resident institutions.

- By residents in foreign currency with non-resident institutions.

Remark: the reservation applies to deposits of funds denominated in foreign currency by an insurance company or a private pension fund with non-resident financial institutions other than those registered in the special section of the National Register of Securities and Intermediaries and of deposits denominated in foreign currency with Mexican financial institutions or foreign financial entities which are affiliates of these. In the case of pension funds such assets may not exceed 70 per cent of mandatory reserves.

NETHERLANDS

*List A, Direct investment:

I/A

    –   In the country concerned by non-residents.

Remark: The reservation applies only to:

i)   *Investment in enterprises operating an airline, unless otherwise implied by the provisions of international agreements to which the Netherlands is a party;*

ii)   *Ownership of Netherlands flag vessels, unless the investment is made by shipping companies incorporated under Netherlands law, established in the Kingdom and having their actual place of management in the Netherlands.*

NEW ZEALAND

List A,   Direct investment:

I/A
- In the country concerned by non-residents.

    Remark: The reservation applies only to:

    i)   *Acquisition of 25 per cent or more of any class of shares or voting power in a New Zealand company where the consideration for the transfer, or the value of the assets, exceeds NZ$ 10 million, unless an authorisation is granted;*

    ii)   *Commencement of business operations, or acquisition of an existing business, in New Zealand, where the total expenditure to be incurred in setting up or acquiring that business exceeds NZ$ 10 million, unless an authorisation is granted;*

    iii)   *Acquisition, regardless of dollar value, of 25 per cent or more of any class of shares or voting power in a New Zealand company engaged in:*

    -   *commercial fishing and*

    -   *rural land;*

    iv)   *Any acquisition, regardless of dollar value, of assets used, or proposed to be used, in a business engaged in any of the activities listed in iii) above.*

    v)   *The registration of vessels to engage in maritime transport activities, except through an enterprise incorporated in New Zealand.*

List B,   Operations in real estate:

III/A1
- In the country concerned by non-residents.

    Remark: *The reservation applies only to the purchase by foreigners (irrespective of their place of residence) of rural farmland, scenic reserve land and off-shore islands.*

List A, Operations in securities on capital markets:

IV/C1
- Purchase in the country concerned by non-residents.

    Remark: The reservation applies only to the purchase of class A shares in Air New Zealand which are reserved to New Zealand nationals.

NORWAY

*List A, Direct investment:

I/A
      – In the country concerned by non-residents.

Remark: The reservation applies only to:

i)   *acquisitions exceeding one-third, one-half or two-thirds of the shares or the voting share capital of an enterprise owning or leasing secondary residences, unless authorisation is granted;*

ii)   *investment in enterprises engaged in the exploration of minerals unless all members of the board of directors are Norwegian nationals;*

iii) *establishment of branches of foreign banks;*

iv) *establishment of branches of securities brokerage firms or management companies for collective investment funds;*

v)   *investment in air transport, except through a limited liability company in which at least two-thirds of the capital is Norwegian;*

vi) *investment in the accountancy sector exceeding 49 per cent, and in the legal sector, by non residents;*

vii) *ownership of Norwegian flag vessels, except a) through a partnership or joint stock company where Norwegian citizens own at least 60 per cent of the capital, b) by registering the vessel in the Norwegian International Ship Register under the applicable conditions;*

viii) *investment in a registered fishing vessel bringing foreign ownership of the vessel above 40 per cent;*

ix) *investment in a nationally operating broadcasting corporation bringing foreign ownership above one-third of the corporation's share capital.*

List B, III/A1	Operations in real estate:

- In the country concerned by non-residents.

   Remark: The reservation applies only to the acquisition of secondary residences by non-residents.

List A, IV/C1	Operations in securities on capital markets:

- Purchase in the country concerned by non-residents.

   Remark: The reservation applies only to the purchase of shares and other securities of a participating nature which may be affected by laws on inward direct investment and establishment.

POLAND

*List A, Direct investment:
I/A
- In the country concerned by non-residents.

  Remark: The reservation applies only to:

  i) *the operation of a branch as a "mortgage bank" to the extent that a "mortgage bank" is defined under Polish law as an institution authorised to issue mortgage securities on domestic markets, and thereby reserved to financial institutions incorporated under domestic law;*

  ii) *the provision of asset management services by branches of non-resident investors to domestic pension funds;*

  iii) *the acquisition of land reserved for agriculture or forests, and acquisition of water areas, unless authorisation is granted;*

  iv) *investment in an enterprise operating an airline, exceeding 49 per cent of the share capital;*

  v) *investment in a broadcasting company bringing foreign ownership of the share capital above 33 per cent;*

  vi) *investment in an enterprise operating in the gambling and betting sector, except through an enterprise incorporated in Poland in which foreign ownership of the capital is 49 per cent or less;*

  vii) *investment in a registered vessel, except through an enterprise incorporated in Poland.*

List B, Operations in real estate:
III/A1,
B1
- In the country concerned by non-residents.

  Remark: The reservation does not apply to the acquisition of apartments, or to foreigners having resided in Poland for at least 5 years.

- Building or purchase abroad by residents.

  Remark: The reservation only applies to the acquisition of real estate abroad by an insurance company.

List A,
IV/B1,
C1, D1

Operations in securities on capital markets:

– Issue through placing or public sale of foreign securities on the domestic capital markct.

Remark: The reservation applies only to mortgage debt securities.

– Purchase of securities in the country concerned by non-residents.

Remark: The reservation applies only to the purchase of shares and other securities of a participating nature, which may be affected by regulations on foreign direct investment.

– Purchase abroad by residents.

Remark: the reservation applies to the purchase of securities issued by non-residents if these assets are to form more than 5 per cent of the cover of the technical reserves of an insurance company or of the assets representative of the liabilities of a privately managed occupational pension fund.

List B,
V/D1

Operations on money markets:

– Purchase abroad by residents.

Remark: the reservation applies to the purchase of securities issued by non-residents if the assets in question are to form more than 5 per cent of the cover of the technical reserves of an insurance company or of the assets representative of the liabilities of a privately managed occupational pension fund.

List B,
VI/D1

Other operations in negotiable instruments on non-securitised claims:

– Purchase abroad by residents.

Remark: the reservation applies to operations in instruments and claims on a foreign market if the assets in question are to form more than 5 per cent of the cover of the technical reserves of an insurance company or of the assets representative of the liabilities of a privately managed occupational pension fund.

List A, VII/D1	Operations in collective investment securities:

List A, VII/D1 — Purchase abroad by residents.

Remark: the reservation applies to the purchase of securities issued by non-residents if the assets in question are to form more than 5 per cent of the cover of the technical reserves of an insurance company or of the assets representative of the liabilities of a privately managed occupational pension fund.

List B, IX/B — Financial credits

— Credits and loans granted by residents to non-residents.

Remark: The reservation applies to:

i) *credits and loans granted by an insurance company if these assets are to form more than 5 per cent of the cover of its technical reserves; or*

ii) *credits and loans granted by a privately managed occupational pension fund.*

List B, XI/B1, B2 — Operation of deposit accounts:

— By residents in domestic currency with non-resident institutions.

Remark: the reservation applies to deposits held with non-resident financial institutions:

i) *by an insurance company if these assets are to form more than 5 per cent of the cover of its technical reserves; or*

ii) *by a privately managed occupational pension fund.*

— By residents in foreign currency with non-resident institutions.

Remark: the reservation applies to deposits held with non-resident financial institutions

i) *by an insurance company if these assets are to form more than 5 per cent of the cover of its technical reserves; or*

ii) *by a privately managed occupational pension fund.*

PORTUGAL

List A,   Direct investment:

I/A, B

- In the country concerned by non-residents.

    Remark: The reservation applies only to:

    i) *creation of a new credit institution or a new financial company owned or controlled by non-EC investors;*

    ii) *establishment of agencies of foreign insurers originating in non-EC Member States for which a special deposit and financial guarantee are required, and whose parent company must have been authorised to exercise such an activity for at least five years;*

    iii) *establishment of enterprises engaged in internal maritime transport, unless the majority of the equity capital is held by Portuguese and the majority of shareholders are Portuguese; and ownership of Portuguese flag vessels other than through an enterprise incorporated in Portugal;*

    iv) *investment by non-EC investors in regular air transport (domestic and international) exceeding 49 per cent of the company's capital;*

    v) *investment in television operations exceeding 15 per cent of capital by a single non-EC investor;*

    vi) *investment exceeding a total of 25 per cent of capital in complementary telecommunications services by non-EC investors;*

    vii) *establishment of travel agencies by non-EC investors except through an enterprise incorporated in Portugal.*

- Abroad by residents.

    Remark: The reservation applies only to:

    i) *establishment in a non-EC Member country of branches of credit institutions and financial companies ("sociedades financieras");*

111

ii)   *establishment in an EC Member country of branches of financial companies ("sociedades financieras") which are not subsidiaries of credit institutions, as defined in Article 18(2) of EC Directive 89/646 of 15 December 1989.*

List B,   Operations in real estate:
III/B1
–   Building or purchase abroad by residents.

Remark: the reservation applies to the acquisition of real estate abroad by a pension fund, which would cause the sum of its foreign assets to exceed 20 per cent of its total assets.

List A,   Operations in securities on capital markets:
IV/B2,
C1, D1   –   Introduction of foreign securities on a recognised domestic securities market.

Remark: The reservation applies only to securities issued by residents of a non-EC Member country and which are not quoted on a recognised market of the issuer's country or of the country in which they are issued.

-   Purchase in the country concerned by non-residents.

Remark: The reservation applies only to the purchase of shares and other securities of a participating nature which may be affected by the laws on inward direct investment and establishment.

-   Purchase abroad by residents.

Remark: the reservation applies to the purchase by a private pension fund of securities issued by non-residents which would cause the sum of its foreign assets to exceed 20 per cent of its total assets.

List B,   Operations on money markets:
V/D1
–   Purchase of money market securities abroad by residents.

Remark: The reservation applies to the purchase by a private pension fund of securities issued by non-residents which would cause the sum of its foreign assets to exceed 20 per cent of its total assets.

List B, VI/D1   Other operations in negotiable instruments and non-securitised claims:

– Purchase abroad by residents.

Remark: the reservation applies to purchase of or swap operations in instruments and claims on a foreign financial market by a private pension fund which would cause the sum of its foreign assets to exceed 20 per cent of its total assets.

List A, VII/D1   Operations in collective investment securities:

– Purchase abroad by residents.

Remark: the reservation applies to the purchase by a private pension fund of securities issued by non-residents which would cause the sum of its foreign assets to exceed 20 per cent of its total assets.

List B, IX/B   Financial credits and loans:

– Credits and loans granted by residents to non-residents.

Remark: the reservation applies to credits and loans granted to non-residents by a private pension fund which would cause the sum of its foreign assets to exceed 20 per cent of its total assets.

List B, XI/B1, B2   Operation of deposit accounts:

- By residents in domestic currency with non-resident institutions.

- By residents in foreign currency with non-resident institutions.

Remark: the reservation applies to deposits of funds by a private pension fund with non-resident financial institutions which would cause the sum of its foreign assets to exceed 20 per cent of its total assets.

SLOVAK REPUBLIC

List A,
I/A

Direct investment:

– In the country concerned by non-residents.

Remark: The reservation applies only to:

i) *the establishment of branches of non-residents in the energy sector;*

ii) *the operation of lotteries and similar games;*

Remark: This reservation does not apply to betting games in casinos for which an authorisation may be granted to legal persons established in the Slovak Republic.

iii) *the purchase of more than 49 percent of the equity capital in air transportation companies.*

List B,
III/A1

Operations in real estate:

– In the country concerned by non-residents.

List B,
IV/A1,
C1

Operations in securities on capital markets:

– Issue through placing or public sale of domestic securities on a foreign capital market.

Remark: The reservation applies only to the issue of municipal debt securities, which is subject to prior approval under the Foreign Exchange Act and implementing regulations under the Debt Securities Act.

– Purchase in the country concerned by non-residents.

Remark: The reservation applies only to the purchase of shares and other securities of a participating nature which may be affected by regulations on inward direct investment in air transport and operations in lotteries and similar games.

List B, XI/B1, B2	Operation of deposit accounts:

- By residents in domestic currency with non-resident institutions.

- By residents in foreign currency with non-resident institutions.

Remark: The reservation does not apply to authorised resident foreign exchange entities, and residents staying abroad for covering the justified operating costs of the resident's local representation or agency abroad, and for the payments of fees, taxes and other documented expenses related to the administration and maintenance of property owned by residents abroad. The reservation will cease to apply on 31 December 2003.

List B, XII/B1, B2, B3	Operations in foreign exchange:

- Purchase of foreign currency with domestic currency abroad by residents.

Remark: The reservation applies only to the purchase of foreign currency with domestic currency not linked to any particular underlying transactions. . The reservation will cease to apply on 31 December 2003.

- Sale of foreign currency for domestic currency abroad by residents.

Remark: The reservation applies only to foreign exchange acquired abroad by residents other than authorised foreign exchange entities and not spent during their stay abroad. The reservation will cease to apply on 31 December 2003.

- Exchange of foreign currencies abroad by residents.

Remark: The reservation applies only to foreign exchange held abroad by residents other than authorised foreign exchange entities and not spent during their stay abroad. The reservation will cease to apply on 31 December 2003.

*List A,   Direct investment:
I/A
- In the country concerned by non-residents.

    Remark: The reservation applies only to:

    i)   *investment originating in non-EC member countries in the following sectors:*

    a)   *air transport;*

    b)   *broadcasting (including television);*

    c)   *telecommunication services other than telephone services;*

    d)   *strategic minerals;*

    e)   *gaming, lotteries, lotto and casinos;*

    f)   *legal services.*

    ii)   *investment originating in non-EC member countries by governments, official institutions, and public enterprises.*

List B,   Operations in real estate:
III/A1,
B1
- In the country concerned by non-residents.

    Remark: the reservation applies to the acquisition of real estate outside the EC if the assets in question are to form part of the cover of the technical reserves of an insurance company.

- Building or purchase abroad by residents.

    Remark: the reservation applies to the acquisition of real estate outside the EC if the assets in question are to form part of the cover of the technical reserves of an insurance company.

List A,   Operations in securities on capital markets:
IV/C1,
D1
- Purchase in the country concerned by non-residents.

    Remark: The reservation applies only to the purchase of shares and other securities of a participating nature which may be affected by laws on inward direct investment and establishment.

– Purchase abroad by residents.

Remark: the reservation only applies to the purchase of securities which are not admitted for trading on a regulated market[1] if the assets in question are to form part of the cover of the technical reserves of an insurance company, except for:

i) *securities issued or guaranteed by international organisations to which an EC member state belongs;*

ii) *fixed income securities provided that a real guarantee or unconditional and several surety has been given on these securities by the credit entity or insurance entity for an insurance, which are authorised to operate through an establishment in an EC member state, or when the shares of the issuing company are traded on a regulated market.*

List B,
V/D1

Operations on money markets:

– Purchase of money market securities abroad by residents.

Remark: the reservation only applies to the purchase of securities which are not admitted for trading on a regulated market if the assets in question are to form part of the cover of the technical reserves of an insurance company, except for:

i) *securities issued or guaranteed by international organisations to which an EC member state belongs;*

ii) *fixed income securities provided that a real guarantee or unconditional and several surety has been given on these securities by the credit entity or insurance entity for an insurance, which are authorised to operate through an establishment in an EC member state, or when the shares of the issuing company are traded on a regulated market.*

---

1. "Regulated market" is understood as any regulated market established in an OECD Member country which fulfils the conditions set out in the EC Directive 93/22/CEE of 10 May 1993 and any other market recognised by the Spanish financial control authorities as applying equivalent standards. (This applies to all references to regulated markets.)

List B, VI/D1 Other operations in negotiable instruments and non-securitised claims:

– Purchase abroad by residents.

Remark: the reservation only applies to operations in instruments and claims on a foreign market if the assets in question are to form part of the cover of the technical reserves of an insurance company, except for:

i) *Mortgage market assets* and *rights issued by companies established in the EC and traded on a regulated OECD market;*

ii) *Bills of exchange and notes when issued, accepted, endorsed without a non-responsibility clause or secured by credit entities authorised to operate through an establishment in the EC. These assets may also be secured by insurance provided by insurance entities which are authorised to operate through an establishment in the EC;*

iii) *Shares of credit entities, brokerage companies and agencies and insurance and reinsurance entities to the extent that they are subject to authorisation and supervision by an EC member state control authority;*

iv) *Derivative instruments, such as options, futures and swaps, in connection with assets representing the technical provisions, to the extent that they help to reduce the investment risk or permit effective management of the portfolio, if traded on a regulated derivatives market, or the counterparts are financial establishments controlled by the EC authorities or subject to the prudential control of supranational bodies to which Spain belongs and they deal habitually and professionally with such transactions and are sufficiently solvent.*

List A, VII/D1 Operations in collective investment securities:

– Purchase abroad by residents.

Remark: the reservation only applies to the holdings of collective investment bodies established outside the EC if the assets in question are to form part of the cover of the technical reserves of an insurance company.

List B, IX/B	Financial credits and loans:

— Credits and loans granted by residents to non-residents.

Remark: the reservation applies to credits and loans granted by residents to non-residents if the assets in question are to form part of the cover of the technical reserves of an insurance company, except for:

i) *credits or quotas-parts thereof granted to companies domiciled in the EC whose shares are admitted for trading on a regulated OECD market;*

ii) *credits secured by a credit entity or insurer authorised to operate through an establishment in an EC member state;*

iii) *financing granted to public corporations of the EC, provided that they offer sufficient guarantee in terms of security, either in the quality of the borrower or of the guarantees provided;*

iv) *mortgage credits, provided these are first mortgages, taken on real estate located in the EC;*

v) *pledge credits, provided that the object of the guarantee is in turn suitable for cover of technical provisions;*

vi) *credits with reinsurers for their participation in the claims provision, to the extent that deposits were not received because of them;*

vii) *credits for interest, income and dividends accrued and not matured, and those which have matured and are pending collection but are not likely not to be collected, provided in all cases that they originate in suitable assets.*

List B, XI/B1, B2	Operation of deposit accounts:

- By residents in domestic currency with non-resident institutions.

- By residents in foreign currency with non-resident institutions.

Remark: the reservation applies to deposits of funds with credit entities established outside the EC, if the assets in question are to form part of the cover of the technical reserves of an insurance company.

List B, XII/B1 Operations in foreign exchange:

- Purchase of foreign currency with domestic currency abroad by residents.

    Remark: the reservation only applies to foreign currencies not traded on an OECD currency market if the assets in question are to form part of the cover of the technical reserves of an insurance company.

SWEDEN

List A,
I/A

Direct investment:

- In the country concerned by non-residents.

    Remark: The reservation applies only to:

    i) *investment to carry out air cabotage and international air transport, and acquisition of aircraft registered in Sweden except through an enterprise incorporated in Sweden;*

    ii) *acquisition of 50 per cent or more of Swedish flag vessels, except through an enterprise incorporated in Sweden;*

    iii) *investment, whether directly or indirectly through residents, in the fields of transport and communications, unless a licence, concession or similar authorisation is granted;*

    iv) *establishment of, or acquisition of 50 per cent or more of shares in, firms engaged in commercial fishing activities in Swedish waters, unless an authorisation is granted;*

    v) *investment in the accountancy sector by non-EC residents exceeding 25 per cent;*

    vi) *investment in a corporation or partnership carrying out the activities of an "advokat" by non-EC residents.[1]*

List B,
III/A1,
B1

Operations in real estate:

- In the country concerned by non-residents.

    Remark: The reservation applies only to the purchase of secondary residences by persons who have not formerly been residents of Sweden for at least five years.

---

1. Unless the Swedish Bar Association grants a waiver, the requirement for EC residency applies for ownership of law firms carrying out business under the title of "advokat".

–   Building or purchase abroad by residents.

Remark: the reservation applies to the acquisition of real estate localised outside Sweden if the asset in question is to form more than 20 per cent of the cover of the technical reserves of an insurance company.

List A, IV/C1, D1
Operations in securities on capital markets:

–   Purchase in the country concerned by non-residents.

Remark: The reservation applies only to shares and other securities of a participating nature which may be affected by laws on inward direct investment in fishing and civil aviation.

–   Purchase abroad by residents.

Remark: the reservation applies to the purchase of securities issued by non-residents if these assets are to form more than 20 per cent of the cover of the technical reserves of an insurance company.

List B, V/D1
Operations on money markets:

–   Purchase of money market securities abroad by residents.

Remark: the reservation applies to the purchase of securities issued by non-residents if these assets are to form more than 20 per cent of the cover of the technical reserves of an insurance company.

List B, VI/D1
Other operations in negotiable instruments and non-securitised claims:

–   Purchase abroad by residents.

Remark: the reservation applies to purchase of or swap operations in instruments and claims issued by or contracted with non-residents if these assets are to form more than 20 per cent of the cover of the technical reserves of an insurance company.

List A, VII/D1
Operations in collective investment securities:

–   Purchase abroad by residents.

Remark: the reservation applies to the purchase of securities issued by non-residents if these assets are to form more than 20 per cent of the cover of the technical reserves of an insurance company.

List B, IX/B   Financial credits and loans:

– Credits and loans granted by residents to non-residents.

Remark: the reservation applies to credits and loans granted to non-residents, if these assets are to form more than 20 per cent of the cover of the technical reserves of an insurance company.

List B, XI/B1, B2   Operation of deposit accounts:

- By residents in domestic currency with non-resident institutions.

- By residents in foreign currency with non-resident institutions.

Remark: the reservation applies to deposits of funds with non-resident financial institutions, if these assets are to form more than 20 per cent of the cover of the technical reserves of an insurance company.

SWITZERLAND

*List A,   Direct investment:
I/A
    –   In the country concerned by non-residents.

    Remark: The reservation applies only to:

    i)   *The establishment of branches for the distribution and exhibition of films;*

    ii)   *The acquisition of real estate, which is subject to authorisation by the competent cantonal authority. As a rule, this authorisation is granted when the acquirer uses the property to operate his permanent establishment;*

    iii)   *The registration of a ship in Switzerland serving two points on the Rhine and of a vessel intended to offer commercial maritime transport services;*

    iv)   *The registration of an aircraft in Switzerland and investment in an airline under Swiss control, unless otherwise implied by the provisions of international agreements to which Switzerland is a party;*

    v)   *Investment in the sectors of hydroelectricity, oil and gas pipelines and nuclear energy;*

    vi)   *Investment in a broadcasting company, bringing foreign ownership above 49 per cent of the company's share capital.*

List B,   Operations in real estate:
III/A1,
B1
    –   In the country concerned by non-residents.

    Remark: The reservation applies only to the acquisition of real estate, which is subject to authorisation by the competent cantonal authority. Authorised acquisitions include purchases of buildings that are used by natural persons as their principal residence or, under certain conditions, secondary residence. In addition, authorisations for holiday homes are subject to quotas. Real estate investments of a purely financial nature are not permitted.

– Building or purchase abroad by residents.

Remark: the reservation applies to the acquisition of real estate localised outside Switzerland, if these assets are to form more than 5 per cent of the cover of the technical reserves of an insurance company or of the assets representative of the liabilities of a private pension fund. Additionally, both insurance companies and pension funds must operate within an overall limit of 30 per cent of total foreign assets allowed as part of mandatory reserves.

List A,
IV/D1

Operations in securities on capital markets:

– Purchase abroad by residents.

Remark: the reservation applies to:

i) *the purchase of debt instruments issued by non-residents if these assets are to form more than 30 per cent of the cover of the technical reserves of an insurance company or of the assets representative of the liabilities of a private pension fund;*

ii) *the purchase of shares or other securities of a participating nature issued by non-residents if these assets are to form more than 25 per cent of the cover of the technical reserves of an insurance company or of the assets representative of the liabilities of a private pension fund.*

Additionally, both insurance companies and pension funds must operate within an overall limit of 30 per cent of total foreign assets allowed as part of mandatory reserves.

List B,
V/D1

Operations on money markets:

Purchase of money market securities abroad by residents.

Remark: the reservation applies to the purchase of debt instruments issued by non-residents if these assets are to form more than 30 per cent of the cover of the technical reserves of an insurance company or of the assets representative of the liabilities of a private pension fund. Additionally, both insurance companies and pension funds must operate within an overall limit of 30 per cent of total foreign assets allowed as part of mandatory reserves.

List B, VI/D1
Other operations in negotiable instruments and non-securitised claims:

– Purchase abroad by residents.

Remark: the reservation applies to purchase of or swap operations in instruments and claims issued by or contracted with non-residents if these assets are to form more than 20 per cent of the cover of the technical reserves of an insurance company or of the assets representative of the liabilities of a private pension fund.

List A, VII/B1, D1
Operations in collective investment securities:

– Issue through placing or public sale of foreign collective investment securities on the domestic securities market.

Remark: The issue of foreign collective investment securities is subject to a stamp duty.

– Purchase abroad by residents.

Remark: the reservation applies to the purchase of securities issued by non-residents if these assets are to form more than 30 per cent of the cover of the technical reserves of an insurance company or of the assets representative of the liabilities of a private pension fund. Additionally, both insurance companies and pension funds must operate within an overall limit of 30 per cent of total foreign assets allowed as part of mandatory reserves.

List B, IX/B
Financial credits and loans:

– Credits and loans granted by residents to non-residents.

Remark: the reservation applies to credits and loans granted to non-residents, if these assets are to form more than 20 per cent of the cover of the technical reserves of an insurance company or of the assets representative of the liabilities of a private pension fund. Additionally, both insurance companies and pension funds must operate within an overall limit of 30 per cent of total foreign assets allowed as part of mandatory reserves.

List B, XI/B1, B2   Operation of deposit accounts:

- By residents in domestic currency with non-resident institutions.

- By residents in foreign currency with non-resident institutions.

    Remark: the reservation applies to deposits of funds with non-resident financial institutions, if these assets are to form more than 30 per cent of the cover of the technical reserves of an insurance company or of the assets representative of the liabilities of a private pension fund. Additionally, both insurance companies and pension funds must operate within an overall limit of 30 per cent of total foreign assets allowed as part of mandatory reserves.

*List A,
I/A, B

Direct investment:

‒ In the country concerned by non-residents.

Remark: The reservation applies only to:

i) *investment in the mining sector, except through a company to be established in Turkey;*

ii) *investment in exploration and exploitation of petroleum by enterprises controlled or owned by foreign states, unless an authorisation is granted;*

iii) *investment in refining, transportation through pipelines and storage of petroleum, unless an authorisation is granted;*

iv) *investment in all sectors, if the value of the investment is less than US$ 50 000;*

v) *investment in the accountancy sector.*

‒ Abroad by residents.

Remark: The reservation applies only to investments exceeding US$ 5 million.

List B,
III/A1,
B1

Operations in real estate:

- In the country concerned by non-residents.

- Building or purchase abroad by residents.

Remark: the reservation applies to the acquisition of real estate localised outside Turkey, if these assets are to form part of the cover of the technical reserves of an insurance company.

List A,
IV/B1,
B2, D1

Operations in securities on capital markets:

‒ Issue through placing or public sale of foreign securities on the domestic securities market.

Remark: The reservation does not apply to:

i) *issues through private placement;*

ii) *shares sold in the form of depository receipts which are issued by non-resident enterprises:*

   a) *in operation since at least 2 years and with declared profits in the last year's financial statements prepared and audited according to international accounting standards; and*

   b) *whose previously issued shares have been quoted for at least one year and traded for at least 100 days before application for public offering in Turkey;*

iii) *debt securities which have at least a medium investment grade rating;*

iv) *securities to be issued on the Istanbul Stock Exchange International Securities Free Zone.*

- Introduction of foreign securities on a recognised domestic securities market.

Remark: The reservation does not apply to:

i) *shares sold in the form of depository receipts which are issued by non-resident enterprises:*

   a) *in operation since at least 2 years and with declared profits in the last year's financial statements prepared and audited according to international accounting standards; and*

   b) *whose previously issued shares have been quoted for at least one year and traded for at least 100 days before application for public offering in Turkey;*

ii) *debt securities which have at least a medium investment grade rating;*

iii) *securities to be issued on the Istanbul Stock Exchange International Securities Free Zone.*

– Purchase abroad by residents.

Remark: the reservation applies to the purchase of securities issued by non-residents if these assets are to form part of the cover of the technical reserves of an insurance company.

List B, V/B1, B2, D1	Operations on money markets:

- Issue through placing or public sale of foreign securities and other instruments on the domestic money market.

  Remark: The reservation does not apply to money market securities which are not regulated under the current legislation on capital markets, such as certificates of deposit and bankers' acceptances.

- Introduction of foreign securities and other instruments on a recognised domestic money market.

  Remark: The reservation does not apply to money market securities which are not regulated under the current legislation on capital markets, such as certificates of deposit and bankers' acceptances.

- Purchase of money market securities abroad by residents.

  Remark: the reservation applies to the purchase of securities issued by non-residents if these assets are to form part of the cover of the technical reserves of an insurance company.

List B, VI/D1	Other operations in negotiable instruments and non-securitised claims:

- Purchase abroad by residents.

  Remark: the reservation applies to purchase of or swap operations in instruments and claims issued by or contracted with non-residents if these assets are to form part of the cover of the technical reserves of an insurance company.

List A, VII/B1, B2, D1	Operations in collective investment securities:

- Issue through placing or public sale of foreign collective investment securities on the domestic securities market.

  Remark: The reservation does not apply to:

  i)   issues through private placement;

  ii) securities issued by foreign unit trusts being at least one year old and generating returns of no less than the average return of comparable unit trusts in their country of origin;

  iii) securities to be issued on the Istanbul Stock Exchange International Securities Free Zone.

– Introduction of foreign collective investment securities on a recognised domestic securities market.

Remark: The reservation does not apply to:

i) *securities issued by foreign unit trusts being at least one year old and generating returns of no less than the average return of comparable unit trusts in their country of origin;*

ii) *securities to be issued on the Istanbul Stock Exchange International Securities Free Zone.*

– Purchase abroad by residents.

Remark: the reservation applies to the purchase of securities issued by non-residents if these assets are to form part of the cover of the technical reserves of an insurance company.

List A, VIII(i)/A, B

Credits directly linked with international commercial transactions or with the rendering of international services in cases where a resident participates in the underlying commercial or service transaction:

- Credits granted by non-residents to residents.

Remark: The reservation applies only to pre-financing credits with a maturity of more than one year.

- Credits granted by residents to non-residents.

Remark: The reservation applies only to commodity credits of more than two years for the export of non-durable goods and of more than five years for the export of other goods.

List B, IX/B

Financial credits and loans:

– Credits and loans granted by residents to non-residents.

Remark: the reservation applies to credits and loans granted to non-residents, if these assets are to form part of the cover of the technical reserves of an insurance company.

List B, XI/B1, B2

Operation of deposit accounts:

- By residents in domestic currency with non-resident institutions.

- By residents in foreign currency with non-resident institutions.

Remark: the reservation applies to deposits of funds with non-resident financial institutions, if these assets are to form part of the cover of the technical reserves of an insurance company.

List B,   Operations in foreign exchange:
XII/B2
-    Sale of foreign currency with domestic currency abroad by residents.

Remark: The reservation applies only to foreign exchange proceeds from merchandise exports of which 70 per cent must be surrendered to authorised resident commercial banks.

UNITED KINGDOM

*List A,   Direct investment:

I/A
  – In the country concerned by non-residents.

    Remark: The reservation applies only to:

    i)   *investment in air transport;*

    ii) *investment in certain broadcasting licences (including, in particular, commercial television, teletext and radio licence) other than by nationals of, or enterprises originating in, EC member countries;*

    iii) *acquisition of United Kingdom flag vessels, except through an enterprise incorporated in the United Kingdom.*

Reservations concerning operations between residents of Bermuda and non-residents:

List A,   Direct investment:

I/A, B
  – In the country concerned by non-residents.

    Remark: The reservation applies only to:

    i)   *investments in enterprises, except hotels, carrying out business inside Bermuda, when the total foreign ownership exceeds 40 per cent of the share capital;*

    ii) *establishment of "exempted companies", (enterprises allowed to carry out business only outside Bermuda) to engage in banking, deposit taking activities, and general management services;*

    iii) *acquisition of real estate, including land, other than hotels;*

    iv) *establishment of branches, agencies, etc. of foreign companies*

  – Abroad by residents.

    Remark: The reservation applies only to resident investment in "exempted companies".

List B, III/A1   Operations in real estate:
–   In the country concerned by non-residents.

List A, IV/C1, D1   Operations in securities on capital markets:
–   Purchase in the country concerned by non-residents.

Remark: The reservation applies to shares or other securities of a participating nature which may be affected by laws on inward direct investment and establishment.

–   Purchase abroad by residents.

Remark: The reservation applies only to the purchase by non-bank residents of securities in excess of the equivalent of BD$ 25 000 per person per annum.

List B, V/D1   Operations on money markets:
–   Purchase of money market securities abroad by residents.

Remark: The reservation applies only to the purchase by non-bank residents of securities in excess of the equivalent of BD$ 25 000 per person per annum.

List B, VI/D1   Other operations in negotiable instruments and non-securitised claims:
–   Purchase abroad by residents.

Remark: The reservation applies only to the purchase by non-bank residents of instruments in excess of the equivalent of BD$ 25 000 per person per annum.

List A, VII/D1   Operations in collective investment securities:
–   Purchase abroad by residents.

Remark: The reservation applies only to the purchase by non-bank residents of securities in excess of the equivalent of BD$ 25 000 per person per annum.

List B, XI/B1, B2   Operation of deposit accounts:
-   By residents in domestic currency with non-resident institutions.
-   By residents in foreign currency with non-resident institutions.

Remark: The reservation applies only to deposits by non-bank residents in excess of the equivalent of BD$ 25 000 per person per annum.

Reservations concerning operations between residents of the Channel Islands and non-residents:

List A,   Direct investment:

I/A
 – In the country concerned by non-residents.

Remark: The reservation applies only to:

i)   *the acquisition in Alderney of real property by non-EC nationals and enterprises originating from non-EC countries, unless an authorisation is granted or the investor is forming or investing in a land-owning company;*

ii) *the ownership in Sark of tenements, which is reserved to British nationals;*

iii) *the purchase in Jersey of real estate, unless economic and social needs tests are satisfied or real estate is acquired through the purchase of shares in a property holding company.*

List B,   Operations in real estate:

III/A1
 – In the country concerned by non-residents.

Remark: The reservation applies only to:

i)   *the acquisition in Alderney of real property by non-EC nationals and enterprises originating from non-EC countries, unless an authorisation is granted or the investor is forming or investing in a land-owning company;*

ii) *the ownership in Sark of tenements, which is reserved to British nationals;*

iii) *the purchase in Jersey of real estate, unless economic and social needs tests are satisfied or real estate is acquired through the purchase of shares in a property holding company.*

UNITED STATES

List A, Direct investment:
I/A
 – In the country concerned by non-residents.

   Remark: The reservation applies only to investment in:

   i) *atomic energy;*

   ii) *broadcasting (radio and television), common carrier, aeronautical en route, or aeronautical fixed radio station licences, unless an authorisation is granted, and the Communications Satellite Corporation;*

   iii) *air transport;*

   iv) *coastal and domestic shipping (including dredging and salvaging in coastal waters and transporting offshore supplies from a point within the United States to an offshore drilling rig or platform on the continental shelf);*

   v) *ocean thermal energy, hydroelectric power, geothermal steam or related resources on federal lands, mining on federal lands or on the outer continental shelf or on the deep seabed, fishing in the "Exclusive Economic Zone", and deepwater ports, except through an enterprise incorporated in the United States.*

List A, Operations in securities on capital markets:
IV/B1,
B2   – Issue through placing or public sale of foreign securities on the domestic capital market.

   Remark: The reservation applies only to the use of small business registration forms and a small issues exemption by non-resident issuers.

 – Introduction of foreign securities on a recognised domestic capital market.

   Remark: The reservation applies only to the use of small business registration forms and a small issues exemption by non-resident issuers.

Decision of the Council Regarding the Application of the Provisions of the Code Of Liberalisation of Capital Movements to Action Taken by the States of the United States

THE COUNCIL,

Having regard to Articles 2(d) and 5(a) of the Convention on the Organisation for Economic Co-operation and Development of 14th December 1960;

Having regard to the Code of Liberalisation of Capital Movements (hereinafter called the "Code");

Having regard to the Report of the Committee for Invisible Transactions on the Codes of Liberalisation of Current Invisible Operations and of Capital Movements of 28th October 1961, in particular, paragraphs 18 to 21 thereof, and the Comments by the Executive Committee on that Report of 8th December 1961 [OECD/C(61)37, OECD/C(61)73];

Recognising that in the United States individual States have jurisdiction to act with respect to certain matters which fall within the purview of the Code;

Believing, however, that there is only a limited area of capital movements in which a Member might consider that the benefits it could reasonably expect to derive from the Code are being denied to it by such action and believing, moreover, that cases of any such action are unlikely to have a significant practical effect on the operation of the Code;

Convinced that where instances of this nature arise they will be settled in the tradition of co-operation which has evolved among the Members of the Organisation;

DECIDES:

1.   The provisions of the Code shall not apply to action by a State of the United States which comes within the jurisdiction of that State.

ACKNOWLEDGES THAT:

2.   a)   If a Member considers that its interests under the Code are being prejudiced by such action and notifies the Organisation of the circumstances, the United States Government undertakes in conformity with the constitutional procedures of the United States to bring the provisions of the Code and the circumstances notified, with an appropriate recommendation, to the attention of the competent authorities of any State concerned;

           b)   The United States Government undertakes to inform the Organisation of the action it has taken pursuant to paragraph 2(a) of this Decision and of the results thereof.

DECIDES:

3.   This Decision shall form an integral part of the Code and shall be attached thereto as Annex C.

Annex D

General List of International Capital Movements and Certain Related Operations[1]

Introduction

1.   The General List is an attempt to establish a comprehensive catalogue of non-governmental operations involving the transfer of capital from one country to another. It also contains certain sections -- concerning, for example, non-resident-owned blocked funds -- under which no such transfers take place but which are nevertheless closely related to the subject-matter of international capital movements for private account.

2.   The general list serves as the basis for the Liberalisation Lists of Capital Movements set out in Annex A to the Code of Liberalisation of Capital Movements, but it does not deal with liberalisation as such. Member countries assume liberalisation obligations only with regard to the operations listed in Annex A to the Code.

3.   The General List enumerates operations which comprise transactions between residents of different countries as well as any capital transfers resulting directly therefrom and envisaged thereunder by the parties concerned. For example, the sections dealing with the granting of credits or loans cover not only the initial transfer of the capital amounts in question but also their subsequent retransfer; they do not, however, cover transfers, such as interest, which are considered to be current payments and therefore are dealt with in the Code of Liberalisation of Current Invisible Operations. The purchase or sale of foreign exchange in order to complete an operation included in the General List is covered by the section dealing with that operation. Foreign exchange transactions that are necessary to complete an operation included in the Code of Liberalisation of Current Invisible Operations are covered by the provisions of that Code.

4.   All international capital movements have two distinct aspects: the capital export from one country and the corresponding capital import into another. Moreover, an operation between residents and non-residents may take

place in the country of the resident, in the country of the non-resident, or in a third country. The attitude to any particular operation of the authorities of the countries concerned may thus differ, and the sections in the General List have been designed to take this into account.

5. Certain international capital operations might be for the account of one and the same person in which case they need not entail transactions between residents and non-residents, e.g. transfers of emigrants' assets, physical movements of capital assets, transfers of blocked funds.

6. The operations enumerated in the General List may be denominated or settled in any currency, including a composite currency such as the ECU or the SDR.

I.   Direct investment

Investment for the purpose of establishing lasting economic relations with an undertaking such as, in particular, investments which give the possibility of exercising an effective influence on the management thereof:

A.   In the country concerned by non-residents by means of:

1.   Creation or extension of a wholly-owned enterprise, subsidiary or branch, acquisition of full ownership of an existing enterprise;

2.   Participation in a new or existing enterprise;

3.   A loan of five years or longer.

B.   Abroad by residents by means of:

1.   Creation or extension of a wholly-owned enterprise, subsidiary or branch, acquisition of full ownership of an existing enterprise;

2.   Participation in a new or existing enterprise;

3.   A loan of five years or longer.

II.   Liquidation of direct investment

A.   Abroad by residents.

B.   In the country concerned by non-residents.

III. Operations in real estate[2]

A. Operations in the country concerned by non-residents:

    1. Building or purchase.

    2. Sale.

B. Operations abroad by residents:

    1. Building or purchase.

    2. Sale.

IV. Operations in securities on capital markets[3]

A. Admission of domestic securities on a foreign capital market:

    1. Issue through placing or public sale of

    2. Introduction on a recognised domestic security market of

    } a) shares or other securities of a participating nature;

    b) bonds and other debt securities (original maturity of one year or more).

B. Admission of foreign securities on the domestic capital market:

    1. Issue through placing or public sale of

    2. Introduction on a recognised domestic security market of

    } a) shares or other securities of a participating nature;

    b) bonds and other debt securities (original maturity of one year or more).

C. Operations in the country concerned by non-residents:

    1. Purchase

    2. Sale

    } a) shares or other securities of a participating nature;

    b) bonds and other debt securities (original maturity of one year or more).

D.   Operations abroad by residents:

1.   Purchase   a)   shares or other securities of a
2.   Sale   }   participating nature;

                           b)   bonds and other debt securities (original maturity of one year or more).

V.   Operations on money markets[4]

A.   Admission of domestic securities and other instruments on a foreign money market:

1.   Issue through placing or public sale.

2.   Introduction on a recognised foreign money market.

B.   Admission of foreign securities and other instruments on the domestic money market:

1.   Issue through placing or public sale.

2.   Introduction on a recognised domestic money market.

C.   Operations in the country concerned by non-residents:

1.   Purchase of money market securities.

2.   Sale of money market securities.

3.   Lending through other money market instruments.

4.   Borrowing through other money market instruments.

D.   Operations abroad by residents:

1.   Purchase of money market securities.

2.   Sale of money market securities.

3.   Lending through other money market instruments.

4.   Borrowing through other money market instruments.

VI. Other operations in negotiable instruments and non-securitised claims[5]

A. Admission of domestic instruments and claims on a foreign financial market:

   1. Issue through placing or public sale.

   2. Introduction on a recognised foreign financial market.

B. Admission of foreign instruments and claims on a domestic financial market:

   1. Issue through placing or public sale.

   2. Introduction on a recognised domestic financial market.

C. Operations in the country concerned by non-residents.

   1. Purchase.

   2. Sale.

   3. Exchange for other assets.

D. Operations abroad by residents:

   1. Purchase.

   2. Sale.

   3. Exchange for other assets.

VII. Operations in collective investment securities

A. Admission of domestic collective investment securities on a foreign securities market:

   1. Issue through placing or public sale.

   2. Introduction on a recognised foreign securities market.

B.   Admission of foreign collective investment securities on the domestic securities market:

1.   Issue through placing or public sale.

2.   Introduction on a recognised domestic securities market.

C.   Operations in the country concerned by non-residents:

1.   Purchase.

2.   Sale.

D.   Operations abroad by residents:

1.   Purchase.

2.   Sale.

VIII. Credits directly linked with international commercial transactions or with the rendering of international services

   i)   In cases where a resident participates in the underlying commercial or service transaction;

   ii)   In cases where no resident participates in the underlying commercial or service transaction.

A.   Credits granted by non-residents to residents.

B.   Credits granted by residents to non-residents.

IX. Financial credits and loans[6]

A.   Credits and loans granted by non-residents to residents.

B.   Credits and loans granted by residents to non-residents.

X.   Sureties, guarantees and financial back-up facilities

i)   In cases directly related to international trade or international current invisible operations, or in cases related to international capital movement operations in which a resident participates;

ii)   In cases not directly related to international trade, international current invisible operations or international capital movement operations, or where no resident participates in the underlying international operation concerned.

A.   Sureties and guarantees:

1.   By non-residents in favour of residents.

2.   By residents in favour of non-residents.

B.   Financial back-up facilities:

1.   By non-residents in favour of residents.

2.   By residents in favour of non-residents.

XI.   Operation of deposit accounts[7]

A.   Operation by non-residents of accounts with resident institutions:

1.   In domestic currency.

2.   In foreign currency.

B.   Operation by residents of accounts with non-resident institutions:

1.   In domestic currency.

2.   In foreign currency.

XII.   Operations in foreign exchange[8]

A.   In the country concerned by non-residents:

1.   Purchase of domestic currency with foreign currency.

2. Sale of domestic currency for foreign currency.

3. Exchange of foreign currencies.

B. Abroad by residents:

1. Purchase of foreign currency with domestic currency.

2. Sale of foreign currency for domestic currency.

3. Exchange of foreign currencies.

XIII. Life assurance

Capital transfers arising under life assurance contracts[9]:

A. Transfers of capital and annuities certain due to resident beneficiaries from non-resident insurers.

B. Transfers of capital and annuities certain due to non-resident beneficiaries from resident insurers.

XIV. Personal capital movements

A. Loans.

B. Gifts and endowments.

C. Dowries.

D. Inheritances and legacies.

E. Settlement of debts in their country of origin by immigrants.

F. Emigrants' assets.

G. Gaming.

H. Savings of non-resident workers.

XV. Physical movement of capital assets

A.   Securities and other documents of title to capital assets:

1.   Import.
2.   Export.

B.   Means of payment:

1.   Import.
2.   Export.

XVI. Disposal of non-resident-owned blocked funds

A.   Transfer of blocked funds.

B.   Use of blocked funds in the country concerned:

1. For operations of a capital nature.
2. For current operations.

C.   Cession of blocked funds between non-residents.

Notes to Annex D

1.   All items on this General List of International Capital Movements and Certain Related Operations appear also on Liberalisation List A or B in Annex A to the Code.

2.   Other than operations falling under Sections I or II of the General List.

3.   Other than operations falling under Sections I or II of the General List.

4.   Other than operations falling under Section IV of the General List.

5.   Other than operations falling under Sections IV, V or VII of the General List.

6.   Other than credits and loans falling under Sections I, II, VIII or XIV of the General List.

7.   Other than operations falling under Section V of the General List.

8.   Other than operations falling under any other Section of the General List.

9.   Transfers of premiums and pensions and annuities, other than annuities certain, in connection with life assurance contracts are governed by the Code of Liberalisation of Current Invisible Operations (Item D/3). Transfers of whatever kind or size under other than life assurance contracts are always considered to be of a current nature and are consequently governed by the Current Invisibles Code.

Decision of the Council regarding measures and practices concerning reciprocity and/or involving discrimination among investors originating in various OECD Member countries in the area of inward direct investment and establishment

THE COUNCIL,

Having regard to Article 5 (a) of the Convention on the Organisation for Economic Co-operation and Development of 14th December 1960;

Having regard to the Code of Liberalisation of Capital Movements (hereinafter called the "Code");

Having regard to the Decision of the Council, of 4th April 1984, amending Annex A to the Code [C(83)106/FINAL];

Having regard to the report by the Committee on Capital Movements and Invisible Transactions of 12th June 1986 on Member countries' positions under the amended obligations concerning the inward direct investment item of the Code [C(86)89 and Corrigenda 1 and 2] and, in particular, paragraphs 10-14 thereof;

On the proposal of the Committee on Capital Movements and Invisible Transactions;

I.		NOTES that some Member countries allow inward direct investment or establishment under conditions of reciprocity (*i.e.* allowing residents of another Member country to invest or establish in the Member country concerned under terms similar to those applied by the other Member country to investors resident in the Member country concerned) and/or involving discrimination among investors originating in various OECD Member countries, other than the exceptions to the principle of non-discrimination referred to in Article 10 of the Code;

II.   RECOGNISES that reciprocity has operated with other factors, in certain cases at least until now, to broaden the effective sphere of liberalisation.

III.   REAFFIRMS, nevertheless, that a more extensive use of reciprocal and/or discriminatory approaches in matters pertaining to inward direct investment or the right of establishment (other than those relating to the exceptions to the principle of non-discrimination referred to in Article 10 of the Code) could reduce the effective sphere of liberalisation among Member countries.

IV.   REAFFIRMS also the importance of the principles underlying Article 8 of the Code concerning the right of each Member country to benefit from measures of liberalisation taken by other Member countries, and of the principles underlying Article 9 of the Code concerning the obligation of each Member country to avoid discrimination between other Members in matters relating to the Code.

V.   RECOGNISES, nevertheless, the right of each Member country under Article 2 of the Code to refrain from immediately bringing their measures and practices into line with the new obligations concerning the right of establishment introduced by the Council Decision of 4th April 1984, referred to above.

VI.   CONSIDERS that, while the status of measures and practices concerning reciprocity and/or involving discrimination among investors originating in various OECD Member countries (other than the exceptions to the principle of non-discrimination referred to in Article 10 of the Code) should be regarded as different from that of restrictions that can be the subject of reservations in accordance with Article 2 of the Code, the procedures applying to such measures and practices should be those applying to measures that can be the subject of reservations.

VII.   DETERMINES that the adoption of this Decision concerning the application of item I/A of the Code on inward direct investment and establishment shall not in any way create a precedent for the application of other items of the Code.

VIII. DECIDES:

1.   All measures and practices concerning reciprocity and/or involving an element of discrimination concerning inward direct investment or establishment (other than the exceptions to the principle of non-discrimination referred to in Article 10 of the Code) and existing as of the date this Decision is adopted shall have been notified to the Organisation. They are recorded in paragraph 5 of this Decision.

2.   Measures and practices recorded in this Decision shall be progressively abolished without, in so doing, extending the scope of restrictions to inward direct investment or establishment. To this end, these measures and practices shall be subject to periodic examination by the Committee on Capital Movements and Invisible Transactions along with the reservations, if any, maintained by the Member countries concerned.

3.   The specific aspects of these measures and practices, including those referred to in paragraphs II and III above, shall be taken into account, particularly when these measures and practices are being examined by the Committee on Capital Movements and Invisible Transactions.

4.   All the other understandings relating to the Code concerning inward direct investment or establishment shall be considered as applying to these measures and practices.

5.   The scope of these measures and practices as notified to the Organisation as of the date of this Decision, is as follows:

AUSTRALIA

Foreign investment in the banking and financial services sectors may be subject to reciprocity considerations.

AUSTRIA

i)   The establishment of branches of foreign securities houses is subject to a reciprocity requirement;

ii)   The establishment of branch offices of insurance companies originating in non-EC countries may be subject to a reciprocity requirement;

iii) The extraction, the preparation and the storing of mass minerals, the running of oil refineries, gasworks, filling stations, district heating, the trading of fuels and pipelines are subject to a reciprocity requirement;

iv) Investment in the transport sector (air transport services, road freight, taxis, buses) is subject to a reciprocity requirement;

v) The establishment of tour operators and travel agencies by non-resident entities is subject to a reciprocity requirement.

BELGIUM

i) Establishment of insurance companies by enterprises originating in non-EC member countries may be subject to a reciprocity requirement;

ii) Establishment of travel agencies by enterprises originating in non-EC member countries is subject to a reciprocity requirement.

CANADA

Establishment of subsidiaries of foreign banks is generally subject to a reciprocity requirement.

General remark: The Canadian authorities undertake to carry out the provisions of this Decision to the fullest extent compatible with the constitutional system of Canada in that the latter provides that individual provinces may have jurisdiction to act with respect to certain matters under the purview of the present Decision. In particular, the authorities undertake to make every effort to ensure that measures for the liberalisation of capital movements pursuant to the present Decision are applied in their provinces; they will notify the Organisation of any relevant measure taken by a province and, if necessary, they will bring to the attention of the provincial authorities any concerns expressed in this respect by a country subscribing to the present Decision.

DENMARK

Establishment of insurance companies originating in non-EC member countries may be subject to a reciprocity requirement.

FINLAND

Foreign investment in the banking and financial services sectors may be subject to reciprocity considerations.

FRANCE

i) Establishment of non-resident investors originating in countries that are not members of the EC in the banking and financial services sector may be subject to reciprocity considerations;

ii) Establishment of insurance companies originating in countries that are not members of the EC may be subject to reciprocity considerations;

iii) Investment by non-EC residents in political and general information publications appearing at least once per month (other than those intended for foreign communities in France), audio-visual communication services, insurance brokerage; tour guide-interpreter services; exploration, extracting and exploitation of hydrocarbons, waterfalls and the purchase of agricultural land adjacent to the Swiss border (under the terms of a bilateral agreement dated 31 August 1946), which is generally allowed only for enterprises originating in a country with which France has undertaken international commitments containing a clause of national assimilation or reciprocity.

GERMANY

i) Establishment of branches of foreign credit institutions (including foreign securities houses) by investors from non-EC member countries may be subject to a reciprocity requirement;

ii) Establishment of airline enterprises that have their headquarters abroad may be subject to a reciprocity requirement.

GREECE

i) Establishment in the banking sector by investors originating in non-EC member countries may be subject to a reciprocity requirement;

ii) Establishment of insurance companies originating in non-EC member countries may be a subject to a reciprocity requirement.

iii) Establishment of travel agencies by enterprises originating in non-EC member countries may be subject to a reciprocity requirement.

ICELAND

Establishment of foreign joint stock companies is subject to a reciprocity requirement.

IRELAND

i) Investment in the banking and financial services sectors by investors from non-EC member countries may be subject to reciprocity considerations;

ii) Establishment of branches of insurance companies originating in non-EC member countries may be subject to reciprocity considerations;

iii) Foreign acquisition of shipping vessels registered in Ireland is subject to a reciprocity requirement.

ITALY

i) Establishment of branches of banks originating in non-EC member countries is subject to a reciprocity requirement;

ii) Establishment of insurance companies originating in non-EC member countries is subject to a reciprocity requirement;

iii) Foreign investment in the exploration and exploitation of liquid and gaseous hydrocarbons is subject to a reciprocity requirement;

iv) The granting of licences to tour operators or travel agents who are nationals of non-EC member countries, or to enterprises in such countries, is subject to a reciprocity requirement.

JAPAN

Establishment of banking branches and subsidiaries of foreign banks is subject to a reciprocity requirement.

NETHERLANDS

Foreign investment in the banking and financial services sector by investors originating in non-EC member countries may be subject to a reciprocity requirement.

NORWAY

i) Establishment of subsidiaries of foreign banks may be subject to a reciprocity requirement;

ii) Establishment of branches or agencies of foreign insurance companies may be subject to a reciprocity requirement.

SPAIN

i) Establishment of non-resident investors originating in non-EC member countries in the banking and financial services sector may be subject to a reciprocity requirement;

ii) Establishment of insurance companies originating in non-EC member countries may be subject to a reciprocity requirement.

SWITZERLAND

i) Foreign investment in the banking and financial services sector is subject to a reciprocity requirement;

ii) Foreign investment in broadcasting is subject to a reciprocity requirement.

TURKEY

Foreign investment in the banking and financial services sector other than insurance may be subject to a reciprocity requirement.

UNITED KINGDOM

i) Foreign investment in the banking and financial services sector may be subject to a reciprocity requirement;

ii) Establishment of insurance companies originating in non-EC member countries may be subject to a reciprocity requirement;

iii) Authorisation of mergers and take-overs involving investors from non-EC member countries may be subject to a reciprocity requirement.

UNITED STATES

i) The acquisition by non-residents of a right-of-way for oil or gas pipelines across onshore federal lands, or a lease to develop mineral resources on on-shore federal lands is subject to a reciprocity requirement;

ii) Foreign investment in air freight forwarding and air charter activities is subject to a reciprocity requirement for US-originating traffic;

iii) The granting of cable landing rights to non-resident firms is subject to a reciprocity requirement.

6.   This decision, adopted 16th July 1986, shall appear in the publication "Code of Liberalisation of Capital Movements" under the heading "Annex E".

LIST OF COUNCIL ACTS INCLUDED IN THE PRESENT EDITION OF THE CODE

1. Code of Liberalisation of Capital Movements [OECD/C(61)96], adopted by the Council on 12th December, 1961.

2. C(62)96/FINAL amending Annexes A and B to the Code of Liberalisation of Capital Movements, adopted by the Council on 3rd July, 1962.

3. C(62)97/FINAL amending Annex B to the Code of Liberalisation of Capital Movements, adopted by the Council on 3rd July, 1962.

4. C(63)15/FINAL amending Annex B to the Code of Liberalisation of Current Invisible Operations and Annexes A and B to the Code of Liberalisation of Capital Movements, adopted by the Council on 26th March, 1963.

5. The Memorandum of Understanding between the Organisation for Economic Co-operation and Development and the Government of Japan, of 26th July, 1963 [C(63)112].

6. C(64)85/FINAL amending the Code of Liberalisation of Capital Movements, adopted by the Council on 28th July, 1964.

7. C(65)26/FINAL amending Annex B to the Code of Liberalisation of Capital Movements, adopted by the Council on 13th April, 1965.

8. C(65)54/FINAL amending Annex B to the Code of Liberalisation of Capital Movements, adopted by the Council on 27th July, 1965.

9. C(65)96/FINAL amending Annex B to the Code of Liberalisation of Capital Movements, adopted by the Council on 9th November, 1965.

10. C(66)10/FINAL amending Annex B to the Code of Liberalisation of Capital Movements, adopted by the Council on 15th February 1966.

11.   C(67)49/FINAL amending Annex B to the Code of Liberalisation of Capital Movements, adopted by the Council on 25th July, 1967.

12.   C(67)69/FINAL amending Annex B to the Code of Liberalisation of Capital Movements, adopted by the Council on 25th July, 1967.

13.   C(67)71/FINAL amending Annex B to the Code of Liberalisation of Capital Movements, adopted by the Council on 15th December, 1967.

14.   C(67)136 amending Annex B to the Code of Liberalisation of Capital Movements, adopted by the Council on 15th December, 1967.

15.   C(68)113/FINAL amending Annex B to the Code of Liberalisation of Capital Movements, adopted by the Council on 26th November, 1968.

16.   C(68)178/FINAL amending Annex B to the Code of Liberalisation of Capital Movements, adopted by the Council on 28th January, 1969.

17.   C(68)111/FINAL amending Annex B to the Code of Liberalisation of Current Invisible Operations and Annex B to the Code of Liberalisation of Capital Movements adopted by the Council on 4th February, 1969.

18.   C(69)41/FINAL amending Annex B to the Code of Liberalisation of Capital Movements, adopted by the Council on 18th March, 1969.

19.   C(69)90/FINAL amending Annex B to the Code of Liberalisation of Capital Movements, adopted by the Council on 8th July, 1969.

20.   C(69)134/FINAL amending Annex B to the Code of Liberalisation of Capital Movements, adopted by the Council on 17th November, 1969.

21.   C(69)157/FINAL amending Annex B to the Code of Liberalisation of Current Invisible Operations and Annex B to the Code of Liberalisation of Capital Movements adopted by the Council on 3rd February, 1970.

22.   C(69)176/FINAL amending Annex B to the Code of Liberalisation of Capital Movements, adopted by the Council on 24th February, 1970.

23.   C(70)2/FINAL amending Annex B to the Code of Liberalisation of Capital Movements, adopted by the Council on 10th March, 1970.

24.   C(70)21/FINAL amending Annex B to the Code of Liberalisation of Capital Movements, adopted by the Council on 17th March, 1970.

25.   C(70)100/FINAL amending Annex B to the Code of Liberalisation of Capital Movements, adopted by the Council on 23rd June, 1970.

26.   C(70)126/FINAL amending Annexes A and B to the Code of Liberalisation of Capital Movements, adopted by the Council on 17th September, 1970.

27.   C(70)161/FINAL amending Annex B to the Code of Liberalisation of Capital Movements, adopted by the Council on 3rd November, 1970.

28.   C(70)212/FINAL amending Annex B to the Code of Liberalisation of Capital Movements, adopted by the Council on 23rd February, 1971.

29.   C(71)3/FINAL amending Annex B to the Code of Liberalisation of Capital Movements, adopted by the Council on 23rd February, 1971.

30.   C(71)11/FINAL amending Annex B to the Code of Liberalisation of Capital Movements, adopted by the Council on 23rd February, 1971.

31.   C(71)24/FINAL amending Annex B to the Code of Liberalisation of Capital Movements, adopted by the Council on 30th March, 1971.

32.   C(71)72/FINAL amending Annex B to the Code of Liberalisation of Capital Movements, adopted by the Council on 2nd June, 1971.

33.   C(71)90/FINAL amending Annexes B to the Code of Liberalisation of Current Invisible Operations and to the Code of Liberalisation of Capital Movements, adopted by the Council on 24th May, 1971.

34.   C(71)127/FINAL amending Annex B to the Code of Liberalisation of Capital Movements, adopted by the Council on 7th October, 1971.

35.   C(71)128/FINAL amending Annex B to the Code of Liberalisation of Capital Movements, adopted by the Council on 7th October, 1971.

36.   C(71)177/FINAL amending Annex B to the Code of Liberalisation of Capital Movements, adopted by the Council on 3rd December, 1971.

37.   C(71)178/FINAL amending Annex B to the Code of Liberalisation of Capital Movements, adopted by the Council on 3rd December, 1971.

38.   C(71)203/FINAL amending Annex B to the Code of Liberalisation of Capital Movements, adopted by the Council on 26th January, 1972.

39.   C(71)241/FINAL amending Annex B to the Code of Liberalisation of Capital Movements, adopted by the Council on 22nd February, 1972.

40.   C(72)111/FINAL amending Annex B to the Code of Liberalisation of Capital Movements, adopted by the Council on 9th June, 1972.

41.   C(72)173/FINAL amending Annex B to the Code of Liberalisation of Capital Movements, adopted by the Council on 31st October, 1972.

42.   C(72)208/FINAL amending Annex B to the Code of Liberalisation of Capital Movements, adopted by the Council on 6th February, 1973.

43.   C(73)11/FINAL amending Annex B to the Code of Liberalisation of Capital Movements, adopted by the Council on 27th February, 1973.

44.   C(72)103/FINAL amending the Code of Liberalisation of Capital Movements, adopted by the Council on 27th February, 1973.

45.   C(72)118/FINAL amending the Code of Liberalisation of Capital Movements, adopted by the Council on 27th February, 1973.

46.   C(73)12/FINAL amending the Code of Liberalisation of Current Invisible Operations and the Code of Liberalisation of Capital Movements, adopted by the Council on 27th February, 1973.

47.   C(73)13/FINAL amending Annex B to the Code of Liberalisation of Capital Movements, adopted by the Council on 21st February, 1973.

48.   C(73)49/FINAL amending Annex B to the Code of Liberalisation of Capital Movements, adopted by the Council on 15th May, 1973.

49.   C(73)60/FINAL amending Annex B to the Code of Liberalisation of Current Invisible Operations and Annex B to the Code of Liberalisation of Capital Movements, adopted by the Council on 15th May, 1973.

50.   C(73)91/FINAL amending Annex B to the Code of Liberalisation of Capital Movements, adopted by the Council on 3rd July, 1973.

51.   C(73)119/FINAL amending Annex B to the Code of Liberalisation of Capital Movements, adopted by the Council on 18th September, 1973.

52.   C(73)164/FINAL amending Annex B to the Code of Liberalisation of Capital Movements, adopted by the Council on 16th October, 1973.

53.   C(74)20/FINAL amending Annex B to the Code of Liberalisation of Capital Movements, adopted by the Council on 12th March, 1974.

54.   C(74)10/FINAL amending Annex B to the Code of Liberalisation of Capital Movements, adopted by the Council on 18th April, 1974.

55.   C(74)56/FINAL amending Annex B to the Code of Liberalisation of Capital Movements, adopted by the Council on 18th April, 1974.

56.   C(74)57/FINAL amending Annex B to the Code of Liberalisation of Capital Movements, adopted by the Council on 21st May, 1974.

57.   C(74)39/FINAL amending Annex B to the Code of Liberalisation of Capital Movements, adopted by the Council on 18th June, 1974.

58.   C(74)97/FINAL amending Annex B to the Code of Liberalisation of Capital Movements, adopted by the Council on 18th June, 1974.

59.   C(74)94/FINAL amending Annex B to the Code of Liberalisation of Capital Movements, adopted by the Council on 27th June, 1974.

60.   C(74)95/FINAL amending Annex B to the Code of Liberalisation of Capital Movements, adopted by the Council on 27th June, 1974.

61.   C(74)149/FINAL amending Annex B to the Code of Liberalisation of Capital Movements, adopted by the Council on 22nd November, 1974.

62.   C(74)225/FINAL amending Annex B to the Code of Liberalisation of Capital Movements, adopted by the Council on 9th January, 1975.

63.   C(75)10/FINAL amending Annex B to the Code of Liberalisation of Capital Movements, adopted by the Council on 29th April, 1975.

64.   C(75)13/FINAL amending Annex B to the Code of Liberalisation of Capital Movements, adopted by the Council on 29th April, 1975.

65.   C(75)89 amending Annex B to the Code of Liberalisation of Capital Movements, adopted by the Council on 12th May, 1975.

66. C(75)112/FINAL amending Annex B to the Code of Liberalisation of Capital Movements, adopted by the Council on 19th August, 1975.

67. C(75)172/FINAL amending Annex B to the Code of Liberalisation of Capital Movements, adopted by the Council on 20th November, 1975.

68. C(75)143/FINAL amending Annex B to the Code of Liberalisation of Capital Movements, adopted by the Council on 28th November, 1975.

69. C(76)199/FINAL amending Annex B to the Code of Liberalisation of Capital Movements, adopted by the Council on 30th December, 1976.

70. C(76)160/FINAL amending Annex B to the Code of Liberalisation of Capital Movements, adopted by the Council on 15th February, 1977.

71. C(77)2/FINAL amending Annex B to the Code of Liberalisation of Capital Movements, adopted by the Council on 10th March, 1977.

72. C(77)3/FINAL amending Annex B to the Code of Liberalisation of Capital Movements, adopted by the Council on 11th May, 1977.

73. C(77)15/FINAL amending Annex B to the Code of Liberalisation of Capital Movements, adopted by the Council on 11th May, 1977.

74. C(77)106/FINAL amending Annex B to the Code of Liberalisation of Capital Movements, adopted by the Council on 23rd December, 1977.

75. C(77)172/FINAL amending Annex B to the Code of Liberalisation of Capital Movements, adopted by the Council on 28th February, 1978.

76. C(77)187/FINAL amending Annex B to the Code of Liberalisation of Capital Movements, adopted by the Council on 28th February, 1978.

77. C(77)219/FINAL amending Annex B to the Code of Liberalisation of Capital Movements, adopted by the Council on 28th February, 1978.

78. C(77)220/FINAL amending Annex B to the Code of Liberalisation of Capital Movements, adopted by the Council on 28th February, 1978.

79. C(78)104/FINAL amending the Code of Liberalisation of Current Invisible Operations and the Code of Liberalisation of Capital Movements, adopted by the Council on 7th August, 1978.

80. C(78)132/FINAL amending Annex B to the Code of Liberalisation of Capital Movements, adopted by the Council on 7th August, 1978.

81. C(78)163/FINAL amending Annex B to the Code of Liberalisation of Capital Movements, adopted by the Council on 27th December, 1978.

82. C(78)164/FINAL amending Annex B to the Code of Liberalisation of Capital Movements, adopted by the Council on 27th December, 1978.

83. C(79)14/FINAL amending Annex B to the Code of Liberalisation of Capital Movements, adopted by the Council on 2nd June, 1979.

84. C(79)15/FINAL amending Annex B to the Code of Liberalisation of Capital Movements, adopted by the Council on 2nd June, 1979.

85. C(79)142/FINAL amending Annex B to the Code of Liberalisation of Capital Movements, adopted by the Council on 6th August, 1979.

86. C(79)133/FINAL amending the Code of Liberalisation of Current Invisible Operations and the Code of Liberalisation of Capital Movements, adopted by the Council on 25th September, 1979.

87. C(79)227/FINAL amending Annex B to the Code of Liberalisation of Capital Movements, adopted by the Council on 30th January, 1980.

88. C(79)208/FINAL amending Annex B to the Code of Liberalisation of Capital Movements, adopted by the Council on 25th February, 1980.

89. C(80)21/FINAL amending Annex B to the Code of Liberalisation of Capital Movements, adopted by the Council on 17th April, 1980

90. C(80)22/FINAL amending Annex B to the Code of Liberalisation of Capital Movements, adopted by the Council on 17th April, 1980.

91. C(80)90/FINAL amending Annex B to the Code of Liberalisation of Capital Movements, adopted by the Council on 25th July, 1980.

92. C(80)91/FINAL amending Annex B to the Code of Liberalisation of Capital Movements, adopted by the Council on 25th July, 1980.

93. C(80)28/FINAL amending Annex B to the Code of Liberalisation of Capital Movements, adopted by the Council on 25th August, 1980.

94.   C(80)89/FINAL concerning the Liberalisation of Capital Movements by Greece, adopted by the Council on 28th October, 1980.

95.   C(80)168/FINAL amending Annex B to the Code of Liberalisation of Capital Movements, adopted by the Council on 23rd March, 1981.

96.   C(80)173/FINAL amending Annex B to the Code of Liberalisation of Capital Movements, adopted by the Council on 23rd March, 1981.

97.   C(81)120/FINAL amending Annex B to the Code of Liberalisation of Capital Movements, adopted by the Council on 15th December, 1981.

98.   C(81)146/FINAL amending Annex B to the Code of Liberalisation of Capital Movements, adopted by the Council on 15th December, 1981.

99.   C(81)148/FINAL amending Annex B to the Code of Liberalisation of Capital Movements, adopted by the Council on 15th December, 1981.

100. C/M(81)21, item 222 (e) amending Annex B to the Code of Liberalisation of Capital Movements and Annex B to the Code of Liberalisation of Current Invisible Operations, adopted by the Council on 15th December, 1981.

101. C(81)139/FINAL amending Annex B to the Code of Liberalisation of Capital Movements, adopted by the Council on 16th December, 1981.

102. C(81)140/FINAL amending Annex B to the Code of Liberalisation of Capital Movements, adopted by the Council on 16th December, 1981.

103. C(81)141/FINAL amending Annex B to the Code of Liberalisation of Capital Movements, adopted by the Council on 16th December, 1981.

104. C(81)168/FINAL amending Annex B to the Code of Liberalisation of Capital Movements, adopted by the Council on 16th December, 1981.

105. C(81)100/FINAL amending Annex B to the Code of Liberalisation of Capital Movements, adopted by the Council on 6th April, 1982.

106. C(82)3/FINAL amending Annex B to the Code of Libcralisation of Capital Movements, adopted by the Council on 26th July, 1982.

107. C(82)73/FINAL amending Annex B to the Code of Liberalisation of Capital Movements, adopted by the Council on 23rd August, 1982.

108.　　C(82)103/FINAL amending Annex B to the Code of Liberalisation of Capital Movements, adopted by the Council on 23rd August, 1982.

109.　　C(82)119/FINAL amending Annex B to the Code of Liberalisation of Capital Movements, adopted by the Council on 6th January, 1983.

110.　　C(82)125/FINAL amending Annex B to the Code of Liberalisation of Capital Movements, adopted by the Council on 6th January, 1983.

111.　　C(82)192/FINAL amending Annex B to the Code of Liberalisation of Capital Movements, adopted by the Council on 6th April, 1983.

112.　　C(83)5/FINAL amending Annex B to the Code of Liberalisation of Capital Movements, adopted by the Council on 7th July, 1983.

113.　　C(83)110/FINAL amending Annex B to the Code of Liberalisation of Capital Movements, adopted by the Council on 16th December, 1983.

114.　　C(83)106/FINAL amending Annex A to the Code of Liberalisation of Capital Movements, adopted by the Council on 4th April, 1984.

115.　　C(83)174/FINAL amending Annex B to the Code of Liberalisation of Capital Movements, adopted by the Council on 29th February, 1984.

116.　　C(83)156/FINAL amending Annex B to the Code of Liberalisation of Capital Movements, adopted by the Council on 26th March, 1984.

117.　　C(84)3/FINAL amending Annex B to the Code of Liberalisation of Capital Movements, adopted by the Council on 24th April, 1984.

118.　　C(84)7/FINAL amending Annex B to the Code of Liberalisation of Capital Movements, adopted by the Council on 24th April, 1984.

119.　　C(84)12/FINAL amending Annex B to the Code of Liberalisation of Capital Movements, adopted by the Council on 24th April, 1984.

120.　　C(84)69/FINAL amending Annex B to the Code of Liberalisation of Capital Movements, adopted by the Council on 31st July, 1984.

121.　　C(84)109/FINAL amending Annex B to the Code of Liberalisation of Capital Movements, adopted by the Council on 17th October, 1984.

122.　　C(84)80/FINAL amending Annex B to the Code of Liberalisation of Capital Movements, adopted by the Council on 18th October, 1984.

123. C(84)82/FINAL amending Annex B to the Code of Liberalisation of Capital Movements, adopted by the Council on 18th October, 1984.

124. C(84)106/FINAL amending Annex B to the Code of Liberalisation of Capital Movements, adopted by the Council on 18th October, 1984.

125. C(84)108/FINAL amending Annex B to the Code of Liberalisation of Capital Movements, adopted by the Council on 18th October, 1984.

126. C(84)154/FINAL amending Annex B to the Code of Liberalisation of Capital Movements, adopted by the Council on 28th December, 1984.

127. C(84)165/FINAL amending Annex B to the Code of Liberalisation of Capital Movements, adopted by the Council on 1st July, 1985.

128. C(84)169/FINAL amending Annex B to the Code of Liberalisation of Capital Movements, adopted by the Council on 1st July, 1985.

129. C(85)54/FINAL amending Annex B to the Code of Liberalisation of Capital Movements, adopted by the Council on 1st July, 1985.

130. C(85)57/FINAL amending Annex B to the Code of Liberalisation of Capital Movements, adopted by the Council on 17th-18th July, 1985.

131. C(85)30/FINAL amending Annex B to the Code of Liberalisation of Capital Movements, adopted by the Council on 25th September, 1985.

132. C(85)180/FINAL amending Annex B to the Code of Liberalisation of Capital Movements, adopted by the Council on 24th March, 1986.

133. C(86)12/FINAL amending Annex B to the Code of Liberalisation of Capital Movements, adopted by the Council on 24th March, 1986.

134. C(86)11/FINAL amending Annex B to the Code of Liberalisation of Capital Movements, adopted by the Council on 26th March, 1986.

135. C(86)29/FINAL amending Annex B to the Code of Liberalisation of Capital Movements, adopted by the Council on 7th April, 1986.

136. C(86)86/FINAL amending Annex B to the Code of Liberalisation of Capital Movements, adopted by the Council on 16th July, 1986.

137. C(86)89/FINAL amending Annex B to the Code of Liberalisation of Capital Movements, adopted by the Council on 16th July, 1986.

138. C(86)119 regarding measures and practices concerning reciprocity and/or involving discrimination among investors originating in various OECD Member countries in the area of inward direct investment and establishment, adopted by the Council on 16th July, 1986.

139. C(86)83/FINAL amending Annex B to the Code of Liberalisation of Capital Movements, adopted by the Council on 29th July, 1986.

140. C(86)171/FINAL amending the Code of Liberalisation of Current Invisible Operations and the Code of Liberalisation of Capital Movements, adopted by the Council on 26th November 1986.

141. C(87)25/FINAL amending Annex B to the Code of Liberalisation of Capital Movements, adopted by the Council on 6th March 1987.

142. C(87)6/FINAL amending Annex B to the Code of Liberalisation of Capital Movements, adopted by the Council on 17th March 1987.

143. C(87)33/FINAL amending Annex B to the Code of Liberalisation of Capital Movements, adopted by the Council on 19th June 1987.

144. C(87)71/FINAL amending Annex B to the Code of Liberalisation of Capital Movements and the Decision reproduced in Annex E to the Code, adopted by the Council on 10th July 1987.

145. C(87)158/FINAL amending Annex B to the Code of Liberalisation of Capital Movements, adopted by the Council on 30th December 1987.

146. C(87)159/FINAL amending Annex B to the Code of Liberalisation of Capital Movements, adopted by the Council on 30th December 1987.

147. C(87)160/FINAL amending Annex B to the Code of Liberalisation of Capital Movements, adopted by the Council on 30th December 1987.

148. C(87)161/FINAL amending Annex B to the Code of Liberalisation of Capital Movements, adopted by the Council on 30th December 1987.

149. C(87)140/FINAL amending Annex B to the Code of Liberalisation of Capital Movements, adopted by the Council on 22nd January 1988.

150. C(87)170/FINAL amending Annex B to the Code of Liberalisation of Capital Movements, adopted by the Council on 22nd January 1988.

151.   C(87)180/FINAL amending Annex B and the Decision reproduced in Annex E to the Code of Liberalisation of Capital Movements, adopted by the Council on 22nd January 1988.

152.   C(88)19/FINAL amending Annex B to the Code of Liberalisation of Capital Movements, adopted by the Council on 30th June 1988.

153.   C(88)42/FINAL amending Annex B to the Code of Liberalisation of Capital Movements, adopted by the Council on 30th June 1988.

154.   C(88)64/FINAL amending Annex B to the Code of Liberalisation of Capital Movements, adopted by the Council on 30th June 1988.

155.   C(88)63/FINAL amending Annex B to the Code of Liberalisation of Capital Movements, adopted by the Council on 8th July 1988.

156.   C(88)122/FINAL amending Annex B to the Code of Liberalisation of Capital Movements, adopted by the Council on 29th December 1988.

157.   C(88)147/FINAL amending Annex B to the Code of Liberalisation of Capital Movements, adopted by the Council on 29th December 1988.

158.   C(88)153/FINAL amending Annex B to the Code of Liberalisation of Capital Movements, adopted by the Council on 14th April 1989.

159.   C(89)46/FINAL amending Annex B to the Code of Liberalisation of Capital Movements, adopted by the Council on 27th June 1989.

160.   C(89)57/FINAL amending the Code of Liberalisation of Current Invisible Operations, adopted by the Council on 10th May 1989.

161.   C(89)111/FINAL amending Annex B and the Decision reproduced in Annex E to the Code of Liberalisation of Capital Movements, adopted by the Council on 18th-20th July 1989.

162.   C(89)114/FINAL amending Annex B and the Decision reproduced in Annex E to the Code of Liberalisation of Capital Movements, adopted by the Council on 12th October 1989.

163.   C(89)137/FINAL amending Annex B to the Code of Liberalisation of Capital Movements, adopted by the Council on 12th October 1989.

164.   C(89)138/FINAL amending Annex B to the Code of Liberalisation of Capital Movements, adopted by the Council on 12th October 1989.

165. C(89)178/FINAL amending Annex B and the Decision reproduced in Annex E to the Code of Liberalisation of Capital Movements, adopted by the Council on 26th October 1989.

166. C(89)131/FINAL amending Annex B and the Decision reproduced in Annex E to the Code of Liberalisation of Capital Movements, adopted by the Council on 26th October 1989.

167. C(89)186/FINAL amending Annex B to the Code of Liberalisation of Capital Movements, adopted by the Council on 23rd February 1990.

168. C(90)1/FINAL amending Annex B to the Code of Liberalisation of Capital Movements, adopted by the Council on 14th April 1990.

169. C(90)3/FINAL amending Annex B to the Code of Liberalisation of Capital Movements, adopted by the Council on 14th April 1990.

170. C(90)50/FINAL amending Annex B to the Code of Liberalisation of Capital Movements, adopted by the Council on 12th June 1990.

171. C(90)72/FINAL amending Annex B to the Code of Liberalisation of Capital Movements, adopted by the Council on 27th July 1990.

172. C(90)73/FINAL amending Annex B to the Code of Liberalisation of Capital Movements, adopted by the Council on 27th July 1990.

173. C(90)86/FINAL amending Annex B to the Code of Liberalisation of Capital Movements, adopted by the Council on 27th September 1990.

174. C(90)96/FINAL amending Annex B to the Code of Liberalisation of Capital Movements, adopted by the Council on 27th September 1990.

175. C(90)120/FINAL amending Annex B to the Code of Liberalisation of Capital Movements, adopted by the Council on 23rd October 1990.

176. C(90)122/FINAL amending Annex B to the Code of Liberalisation of Capital Movements, adopted by the Council on 23rd October 1990.

177. C(91)2/FINAL amending Annex B to the Code of Liberalisation of Capital Movements, adopted by the Council on 10th April 1991.

178. C(91)3/FINAL amending Annex B to the Code of Liberalisation of Capital Movements, adopted by the Council on 17th April 1991.

179.   C(91)4/FINAL amending Annex B to the Code of Liberalisation of Capital Movements, adopted by the Council on 12th March 1991.

180.   C(91)7/FINAL amending Annex B to the Code of Liberalisation of Capital Movements, adopted by the Council on 12th March 1991.

181.   C(91)8/FINAL amending Annex B to the Code of Liberalisation of Capital Movements, adopted by the Council on 12th March 1991.

182.   C(91)105/FINAL amending Annex B to the Code of Liberalisation of Capital Movements, adopted by the Council on 12th, 13th, 17th and 19th December 1991.

183.   C(91)160/FINAL amending Annex B to the Code of Liberalisation of Capital Movements, adopted by the Council on 4th February 1992.

184.   C(91)90/FINAL amending Annex B to the Code of Liberalisation of Capital Movements, adopted by the Council on 27th February 1992.

185.   C(92)4/FINAL amending the Code of Liberalisation of Capital Movements, adopted by the Council on 27th February 1992.

186.   C(92)13/FINAL amending the Code of Liberalisation of Capital Movements, adopted by the Council on 12th June 1992.

187.   C(92)58/FINAL amending the Code of Liberalisation of Capital Movements, adopted by the Council on 17th July 1992.

188.   C(92)60/FINAL amending the Code of Liberalisation of Capital Movements, adopted by the Council on 17th July 1992.

189.   C(92)62/FINAL amending the Code of Liberalisation of Capital Movements, adopted by the Council on 23rd July 1992.

190.   C(92)57/FINAL amending the Code of Liberalisation of Capital Movements, adopted by the Council on 23rd September 1992.

191.   C(92)138/FINAL amending the Code of Liberalisation of Capital Movements, adopted by the Council on 24th November 1992.

192.   C(92)170/FINAL amending the Code of Liberalisation of Capital Movements, adopted by the Council on 18th December 1992.

193.   C(92)174/FINAL amending the Code of Liberalisation of Capital Movements, adopted by the Council on 18th December 1992.

194.   C(92)142/FINAL amending the Code of Liberalisation of Capital Movements, adopted by the Council on 18th December 1992.

195.   C(92)219/FINAL amending the Code of Liberalisation of Capital Movements, adopted by the Council on 29th March 1993.

196.   C(92)139/FINAL amending the Code of Liberalisation of Capital Movements, adopted by the Council on 15th April 1993.

197.   C(93)4/FINAL amending the Code of Liberalisation of Capital Movements, adopted by the Council on 9th March 1993.

198.   C(93)7/FINAL amending the Code of Liberalisation of Capital Movements, adopted by the Council on 9th March 1993.

199.   C(93)12/FINAL amending the Code of Liberalisation of Capital Movements, adopted by the Council on 29th March 1993.

200.   C(93)186/FINAL amending the Code of Liberalisation of Capital Movements, adopted by the Council on 1st March, 1993.

201.   C(93)187/FINAL amending the Code of Liberalisation of Capital Movements, adopted by the Council on 1st March, 1994.

202.   C(94)4/FINAL amending the Code of Liberalisation of Capital Movements, adopted by the Council on 15th April, 1994.

203.   C(94)5/FINAL amending the Code of Liberalisation of Capital Movements, adopted by the Council on 15th April, 1994.

204.   C(94)47/FINAL amending the Code of Liberalisation of Capital Movements, adopted by the Council on 10th February, 1995.

205.   C(94)49/FINAL amending the Code of Liberalisation of Capital Movements, adopted by the Council on 14th and 15th April, 1994.

206.   C(94)64/FINAL amending the Code of Liberalisation of Capital Movements, adopted by the Council on 21st April, 1994.

207.   C(94)68/FINAL amending the Code of Liberalisation of Capital Movements, adopted by the Council on 19th May 1994.

208. C(94)83/FINAL amending the Code of Liberalisation of Capital Movements, adopted by the Council on 2d June 1994.

209. C(94)85/FINAL amending the Code of Liberalisation of Capital Movements, adopted by the Council on 29th July 1994.

210. C(94)104/FINAL amending the Code of Liberalisation of Capital Movements, adopted by the Council on 3rd June 1994.

211. C(94)118/FINAL amending the Code of Liberalisation of Capital Movements, adopted by the Council on 5th July 1994.

212. C(94)229/FINAL amending the Code of Liberalisation of Capital Movements, adopted by the Council on 22nd February, 1995.

213. C(94)230/FINAL amending the Code of Liberalisation of Capital Movements, adopted by the Council on 18th April, 1995.

214. C(94)235/FINAL amending the Code of Liberalisation of Capital Movements, adopted by the Council on 10th February, 1995.

215. C(95)4/FINAL amending the Code of Liberalisation of Capital Movements, adopted by the Council on 22nd February, 1995.

216. C(95)23/FINAL amending the Code of Liberalisation of Capital Movements, adopted by the Council on 10th March, 1995.

217. C(95)45/FINAL amending the Code of Liberalisation of Capital Movements, adopted by the Council on 19th April, 1995.

218. C(95)46/FINAL amending the Code of Liberalisation of Capital Movements, adopted by the Council on 19th May, 1995.

219. C(95)48/FINAL amending the Code of Liberalisation of Capital Movements, adopted by the Council on 19th May, 1995.

220. C(95)49/FINAL amending the Code of Liberalisation of Capital Movements, adopted by the Council on 2nd May, 1995.

221. C(95)44/FINAL amending the Code of Liberalisation of Capital Movements, adopted by the Council on 27th June, 1995.

222. C(95)128/FINAL amending the Code of Liberalisation of Capital Movements, adopted by the Council on 20th July, 1995.

223. C(95)188/FINAL amending the Code of Liberalisation of Capital Movements, adopted by the Council on 24th November, 1995.

224. C(95)239/FINAL amending the Code of Liberalisation of Capital Movements, adopted by the Council on 12th February, 1996.

225. C(96)3/FINAL amending the Code of Liberalisation of Capital Movements, adopted by the Council on 12th February, 1996.

226. C(96)19/FINAL amending the Code of Liberalisation of Capital Movements, adopted by the Council on 28th March, 1996.

227. C(96)59/FINAL amending the Code of Liberalisation of Capital Movements, adopted by the Council on 24th May, 1996.

228. C(96)147/FINAL amending the Code of Liberalisation of Capital Movements, adopted by the Council on 22nd November, 1996.

229. C(96)198/FINAL amending the Code of Liberalisation of Capital Movements, adopted by the Council on 28th November, 1996.

230. C(96)199/FINAL amending the Code of Liberalisation of Capital Movements, adopted by the Council on 28th November, 1996.

231. C(96)215/FINAL amending the Code of Liberalisation of Capital Movements, adopted by the Council on 28th November, 1996.

232. C(96)256/FINAL amending the Code of Liberalisation of Capital Movements, adopted by the Council on 12th December, 1996.

233. C(97)51/FINAL amending the Code of Liberalisation of Capital Movements, adopted by the Council on 4th April, 1997.

234. C(97)55/FINAL amending the Code of Liberalisation of Capital Movements, adopted by the Council on 23rd April, 1997.

235. C(97)67/FINAL amending Annex B to the Code of Liberalisation of Capital Movements, adopted by the Council on 23rd April, 1997.

236. C(97)164/FINAL amending Annex B to the Code of Liberalisation of Capital Movements, adopted by the Council on 26 September, 1997.

237. C(98)7/FINAL amending Annex B to the Code of Liberalisation of Capital Movements, adopted by the Council on 26 February, 1998.

238.   C(98)64/FINAL amending Annex B to the Code of Liberalisation of Capital Movements, adopted by the Council on 23rd April 1998.

239.   C(98)90/FINAL amending Annex B to the Code of Liberalisation of Capital Movements, adopted by the Council on 10 September 1998.

240.   C(98)155/FINAL amending Annex B to the Code of Liberalisation of Capital Movements, adopted by the Council on 12 November 1998.

241.   C(99)21/FINAL amending Annex B to the Code of Liberalisation of Capital Movements, adopted by the Council on 18 February 1999.

242.   C(2000)120/FINAL amending Annex B to the Code of Liberalisation of Capital Movements, adopted by the Council on 13 July 2000.

243.   C(2000)123/FINAL amending the Code of Liberalisation of Capital Movements, adopted by the Council on 28 July 2000.

244.   C(2000)128/FINAL amending Annex B to the Code of Liberalisation of Capital Movements, adopted by the Council on 28 July 2000.

245.   C(2000)150/FINAL amending Annex B to the Code of Liberalisation of Capital Movements, adopted by the Council on 28 September 2000.

246.   C(2000)151/FINAL amending Annex B to the Code of Liberalisation of Capital Movements, adopted by the Council on 28 September 2000.

247.   C(2000)158/FINAL amending Annex B to the Code of Liberalisation of Capital Movements, adopted by the Council on 28 September 2000.

248.   C(2000)54 and CORR1 amending Annex B to the Code of Liberalisation of Capital Movements, adopted by the Council on 4 October 2000.

249.   C(2000)121 amending Annex B to the Code of Liberalisation of Capital Movements, adopted by the Council on 4 October 2000.

250.   C(2000)114 amending Annex B to the Code of Liberalisation of Capital Movements, adopted by the Council on 14 December 2000, on the occasion of the Slovak Republic's accession to the OECD.

251.   C(2000)180 amending Annex B to the Code of Liberalisation of Capital Movements, adopted by the Council on 6 November 2000.

252.   C(2001)72 amending Annex B to the Code of Liberalisation of Capital Movements, adopted by the Council on 26 April 2001.

253.   C(2001)241 amending Annex B to the Code of Liberalisation of Capital Movements, adopted by the Council on 28 November 2001.

254.   C(2001)243 amending Annex B to the Code of Liberalisation of Capital Movements, adopted by the Council on 28 November 2001.

255.   C(2001)242 amending Annex B to the Code of Liberalisation of Capital Movements, adopted by the Council on 5 December 2001.

256.   C(2002)30 amending Annex B to the Code of Liberalisation of Capital Movements, adopted by the Council on 28 March 2002.

257.   C(2002)120 amending Annex B to the Code of Liberalisation of Capital Movements, adopted by the Council on 25 July 2002.

258.   C(2002)100 amending Annex B to the Code of Liberalisation of Capital Movements, adopted by the Council on 23 September 2002.

259.   C(2002)233 amending Annex B to the Code of Liberalisation of Capital Movements, adopted by the Council on 12 December 2002.

260.   C(2003)28 amending Annex B to the Code of Liberalisation of Capital Movements, adopted by the Council on 27 March 2003.

OECD PUBLICATIONS, 2, rue André-Pascal, 75775 PARIS CEDEX 16
PRINTED IN FRANCE
(20 2003 01 1 P) ISBN 92-64-19988-8 – No. 52903 2003